Teaching and Working With Children
Who Have Emotional and Behavioral Challenges

Mary Magee Quinn, Ph.D.
David Osher, Ph.D.
Cynthia L. Warger, Ph.D.
Tom V. Hanley, Ed.D.
Beth DeHaven Bader, M.S.
Catherine C. Hoffman, A.B.

ISBN 1-57035-308-5

05 04 03 02 01 00   6 5 4 3 2 1

Edited by Terri Bates Eyden
Text layout and design by Holley VanDenBerg
Cover design by Holley VanDenBerg

Printed in the United States of America
Published and Distributed by

Sopris West
*Helping You Meet the Needs
of At-Risk Students*

4093 Specialty Place
Longmont, Colorado 80504
303-651-2829 • www.sopriswest.com

IDEAs that Work
Office of Special
Education Programs

Dear Educator:

We are very pleased to see the publication of *Teaching and Working With Children Who Have Emotional and Behavioral Challenges*. This new book reflects a continuing commitment by the Office of Special Education Programs (OSEP) to involve all stakeholders in the Department of Education's efforts to ensure that the schools remain safe and effective learning environments for *all* children.

In 1994, we published the *National Agenda for Achieving Better Results for Children and Youth with Serious Emotional Disturbance*. That landmark document resulted from focus groups we conducted around the nation to provide us with a better framework for helping troubled students and their families. One of the messages that we heard over and over, and eventually made into a crosscutting theme of the *National Agenda*, was the urgent need for collaboration across the different agencies and professionals, including teachers, who work with troubled youth. All too often in the past, services have been fragmented; they placed an unnecessary burden on families to sift through the different protocols and procedures from agencies that were not coordinating effectively.

We are changing that pattern. In 1996, OSEP established the Center for Effective Collaboration and Practice, at the American Institutes for Research, to foster the exchange of information on effective practices across agencies at federal, state, and local levels. To do this, the Center has directly involved the major national professional organizations, along with leading researchers and policymakers, to synthesize information and guidance on what truly works. Many of these efforts have been cosponsored by the Center for Mental Health Services in the U.S. Department of Health and Human Services, the Office of Juvenile Justice and Delinquency Prevention in the Department of Education, and by our sister agency in the Department of Education—the Safe and Drug-Free Schools Program. Two other publications that also resulted from these joint efforts are *Early Warning, Timely Response: A Guide to Safe Schools* (1998) and its new companion piece, *Safeguarding Our Children: An Action Guide* (2000).

That is why I am so enthusiastic about this new publication. Where the other documents have been targeted to the broadest audience, we felt it was equally important to pull information together in one book that would be specifically useful and meaningful to the nation's teachers. This is that book. I hope that you enjoy reading it, and that the information it contains will help you increase successful outcomes for your students and contribute to the overall "positivity" of your schools and communities.

— Kenneth Warlick, Director
Office of Special Education Programs
U.S. Department of Education

CENTER FOR EFFECTIVE COLLABORATION AND PRACTICE

Improving Services for Children and Youth with Emotional and Behavioral Problems

Senior Center Staff

David Osher
Director

Stephanie Jackson
Deputy Director

Mary Magee Quinn
Deputy Director

Beth Bader
Kevin Dwyer
Allison Gruner
Kimberly Kendziora
Debra Pacchiano
Erika Taylor
Darren Woodruff

Senior Technical Advisors

James Hamilton
Maurice McInerney

Russell Gersten
Evaluator

Advisory Board

Mary Lynn Cantrell
Positive Education Program

Gail Daniels
Federation of Families
for Children's Mental
Health

Gary DeCarolis
Center for Mental
Health Services

Karl Dennis
Kaleidoscope, Inc.

Michael Faenza
National Mental
Health Association

José Flores
LaFamilia
Counseling Service

Dixie Jordan
PACER Center

Michael Kane
American Institutes
for Research

Frank Wood
University of
Minnesota

Dear Reader:

Successful schools build their capacity to serve all students. These schools are characterized by collaborations among staff—paraprofessionals, teachers, and student service personnel. These educators work and problem solve together, and they employ evidence-based practices to improve results for every student. Models exist for this work (e.g., *National Agenda for Achieving Better Results for Children and Youth with Serious Emotional Disturbance*), and there are many evidence-based practices that school teams can employ. The challenge is to enable educators to identify and employ resources that respond to their needs and those of their students.

Teaching and Working With Students Who Have Emotional and Behavioral Challenges was developed in such a manner. As in its other projects, the Center for Effective Collaboration and Practice (CECP) worked with strategic partners to develop this book. In addition, CECP held meetings, telephone conferences, and focus groups with the educators from regular and special education, who are listed in the Acknowledgments, to conceptualize, design, and review this book. These educators reviewed the *National Agenda* and identified the information that they needed in order to improve results for students with emotional and behavioral challenges.

CECP thanks all those individuals and associations who helped develop this book. Their extensive assistance improved this document at every step. Without their enthusiasm and assistance, this project could never have been brought to fruition. While too numerous to mention by name, we are indebted to all of those who participated for their time and talent. Their efforts should send a strong message to all school districts that the resolution of student behavior problems in U.S. schools must be a collaborative effort that involves special and regular educators, families, and communities in all schools and districts.

David Osher
Director
Center for Effective Collaboration and Practice

AMERICAN INSTITUTES FOR RESEARCH • 1000 Thomas Jefferson St., N. W., Suite 400, Washington, D.C. 20007
Phone (202)944-5300 or 1-888-457-1551 **Fax:** (202)944-5454 **e-mail** center@air.org **Web Site:** www.air.org/cecp

ACKNOWLEDGMENTS

The following are names of people who participated in one or more of the many meetings, telephone conferences, focus groups, review panels, and conversations with the authors, and/or who made comments on the early drafts of the document.

Ed Amundsen—California
Toni Atkinson-Williams—Washington, DC
Sundy Barjon—Louisiana
Vinoo Bawa—Virginia
Allen Bearden—Illinois
Gregory Bolton—Virginia
Linda Burnett—Washington, DC
Denise Casar—Ohio
Marian Ceasor—Washington, DC
Ivy Chan—California
Denise Conrad—Ohio
Mary Davenport—Texas
Romona Davis—Louisiana
Mary Beth Doherty—Maine
Terry Edelstein—Washington, DC
Molly Effland—Oklahoma
Marian Fast—Pennsylvania
Grace Fitzpatrick—Massachusetts
Marilyn Greene—Washington, DC
Barbara Hardy—Virginia
Leon Horne—Washington

Ted Hughes—Texas
Cynthia Jefferson—Pennsylvania
Valerie Johnson Powell—Kansas
Jeanne Louizos—Massachusetts
Sean McLaughlin—Maryland
Andrea Mattia—Rhode Island
Barbara Meranus—New York
Susie Oleson—Connecticut
Garrett Panzer—Kansas
Lucille Pazienza—Rhode Island
Jennifer Penn—Washington, DC
Julie Pope—Oregon
Diane Porter—Florida
Patty Ralabate—Connecticut
Janet Rice—Maryland
Kathy Riley—Ohio
Marta Rovira—Virginia
Richard Simmons—Illinois
Jeff Timmons—Texas
Vernetta Tupa—Ohio
Sue Walter—Illinois

About
THE AUTHORS

Mary Magee Quinn, a Senior Research Scientist at the American Institutes for Research (AIR), is a Deputy Director of the Center for Effective Collaboration and Practice (CECP). She has worked extensively with the researchers whose work provides the foundation for this book. Dr. Quinn has extensive experience as a teacher of children with emotional disturbances and with learning disabilities in the United States and for the Department of Defense Dependent Schools. Dr. Quinn also has designed and taught numerous inservice training modules for teachers, paraprofessionals, and school-related personnel on providing appropriate services to children with emotional or behavioral problems and their families. She is experienced in designing and conducting research and providing evidence-based technical assistance. She has been with CECP for four years and has been central to the many related activities of CECP. Her work has been published in professional journals, and she has made many presentations at national and international conferences. She also has served as a guest reviewer for journals and monographs such as *Behavioral Disorders* and *Education and Treatment of Children.* She is currently a field reviewer for *Preventing School Failure* and the *Journal of Emotional and Behavioral Disorders.* Quinn received her Ph.D. in special education from Arizona State University in Tempe, Arizona.

David Osher, a Managing Associate at the American Institutes for Research, is the Director of the Center for Effective Collaboration and Practice. Dr. Osher focuses his work on knowledge use, violence prevention, schoolwide and community-wide interventions for youth with emotional and behavioral disorders and their families, and building meaningful collaborations at federal, state, and local levels. He has been an active and vocal advocate for children with emotional and/or behavioral problems and their families for over 20 years. In addition, he is the parent of two children with disabilities. Dr. Osher has consulted with the U.S. Departments of Education and Health and Human Services, the Office of Juvenile Justice and Delinquency Prevention, the National Institute for Literacy, as well as with public officials and agency staff in many states and communities. He is a contributing editor on numerous professional journals, including the *Journal of Emotional and Behavioral Disorders* and *Reaching Today's Youth,* and he serves as an advisory board member and consultant to a variety of organizations, typified by the Mental Health Advisory Board of the Child Welfare League, the Technical Assistance Center for Professional Development Partnership Projects, and the Center for Policy Options in Special Education. His work has been published in professional and family-oriented journals and newsletters, and he has made countless presentations across the United States to a vast array of audiences, including policy makers, practitioners, researchers, and family members. Before coming to AIR, Osher was dean of a liberal arts college and of two schools of human services. Osher received his A.B., A.M., and Ph.D. from Columbia University.

Cynthia L. Warger is principal of Warger, Eavy & Associates, a communications firm in Reston, Virginia, that specializes in education print and media. Dr. Warger received her Ph.D. in educational psychology from the University of Michigan and an M.S. in special education, with emphasis on emotional disturbance. She has taught in the public schools, directed teacher education programs at the university level, and served as an education association executive. While editor of *Teaching Exceptional Children,* she won national EdPress awards for excellence. She is coauthor with David Osher and Kevin Dwyer on *Early Warning, Timely Response: A Guide to Safe Schools.* A recent video, *Promising Practices for Safe and Effective Schools,* which aired as part of a federally sponsored teleconference, won a Communicator Award of Excellence. She is a past president of the International Council for Children with Behavior Disorders.

Tom V. Hanley, an educational psychologist with experience in special education, educational research and evaluation; computer programming and systems development; statistical analysis; survey research and sampling; and computer applications in education. He is currently with the U.S. Department of Education, Office of Special Education and Rehabilitation Services (OSERS), Office of Special Education Programs (OSEP). In the Research to Practice Division, Dr. Hanley coordinates research programs and special projects for children with emotional and behavioral problems, administrates the Field Initiated and Directed Research Programs, manages the OSEP Standing Panel, and provides statistical analyses for all discretionary grant competitions. Dr. Hanley has been a principal research scientist on many federal studies related to programs and services for individuals with disabilities. He is extensively involved in issues related to improving services for children with emotional and behavioral needs, and to effective applications of innovative technologies to improve instruction. Dr. Hanley received his Ed.D. from Rutgers University in 1979.

Beth DeHaven Bader is a Senior Research Analyst with AIR. Ms. Bader is an experienced professional developer with seven years of experience in adult instruction and six years of experience in the classroom. Bader has a broad knowledge of the research foundations of the material in this book, extensive contacts with the researchers who conducted this research, and considerable experience in both professional development and converting research to practice. Ms. Bader has also served on a number of advisory panels for research and practice projects, including Interstate New Teacher Assessment and Support Consortium's project to determine appropriate standards for general education teachers who teach disabled students. She received her M.S. in education from the University of Pennsylvania in Philadelphia.

Catherine C. Hoffman, Research Associate at AIR, is the Project Coordinator for CECP. A former educator, Ms. Hoffman is knowledgeable about both policy issues and effective practices for children with serious emotional disturbance. As part of her work with CECP, she coauthored *Safe and Effective Schools for ALL Students: What Works!,* a report prepared for a collaboration between the Office of Special Education Programs (OSEP) and the Safe and Drug-Free Schools Program. She also coauthored *The Role of Education in a System of Care: Effectively Serving Children with Emotional and Behavioral Disorders,* the third volume in the Center for Mental Health Services' series on *Systems of Care: Promising Practices in Children's Mental Health.* She has also participated in research into functional behavioral assessment techniques and coauthored *Addressing Student Problem Behavior—Part II: Conducting a Functional Assessment.* Ms. Hoffman holds an A.B. from Bryn Mawr College and is a certified teacher in the Commonwealth of Pennsylvania. She has been working on disability and mental health issues at AIR since 1996.

CONTENTS

Chapter 1

OVERVIEW

Clark, an eight-year-old student with learning disabilities and emotional and behavior disorders, has been placed in a regular third grade class of 30 students. The classroom is managed by one teacher, Ms. Cameron, who was not able to attend Clark's IEP (individualized education program) meeting due to a lack of classroom coverage. No paraprofessional is available to help Clark make the transition into the regular classroom or to assist with his academic and behavioral needs.

Ms. Cameron reports that while Clark is a bright student, his learning difficulties and behavior problems have caused him to fall well behind in his studies, particularly in math. While most of his classmates were at grade level in math when they entered third grade, Clark was functioning at first grade level. Although Ms. Cameron has tried a number of strategies to assist Clark, he has not responded well to them. Further, for half the year, Clark has been seriously disruptive during the math lesson. He refuses to do his work, calls out and makes loud noises, throws pencils across the room, and tears up his classmates' papers.

Repeated trips to the principal's office and calls home to Clark's parents have been of no consequence. Because he has an IEP, the principal believes that Clark cannot be disciplined. His parents are reluctant to allow him to be placed back in a special education classroom, even part time for math class.

Ms. Cameron is particularly worried because Clark's disruptive behavior is causing her to fall behind in teaching academic lessons. This means that the other students are also falling behind, as Clark fails to make progress. In addition, Clark's classmates are angry about his constant disruptions. They are becoming less tolerant of his disabilities rather than more tolerant, refusing to sit next to him and avoiding him during recess. Ms. Cameron worries daily about how Clark's behavior is affecting learning in her classroom.

Most teachers can tell stories of their own "Clark." In fact, students like Clark challenge best practices and contribute their own brand of worry and stress to adults and other students. Teachers care about such students, but they also care about others' and their own peace of mind. Many educators—administrators, teachers, paraprofessionals, related service providers, and other school staff—as well as the parents of these children are left wondering what to do.

It goes without saying that there are no easy answers or quick fixes when working with students with emotional and behavioral problems. However, over the years, educators and families have accumulated a wealth of information about how to work with these students. While there is

This chapter provides an overview of the needs and problems presented by students who have emotional and behavioral challenges as well as the ways those needs and challenges can be addressed.

much that remains unknown, both practitioners and researchers have much to say about how to provide learning opportunities for such students. For every "Clark," practitioners have found a way to reach a "Trisha" or a "Clyde" or a "Charles."

This book addresses challenging behaviors and describes effective methods for providing positive supports to the students who have them. The book was developed to help educators—teachers, paraprofessionals, related service providers, and others—who work with students who have emotional and behavioral challenges.

▬▬▬ Special Considerations for Students With Disabilities Who Have Behavioral Challenges

Some of these children are eligible to receive special education and related services under the Individuals with Disabilities Education Act (IDEA) if their disability meets the requirements of the law (under the "emotional disturbance" or other categories of disability classification). However, many others—including some who may be "at risk" of emotional disturbance if they do not receive appropriate early intervention and prevention services—are not eligible for special education services. Consequently, the wording used in this book, "students with emotional and behavioral challenges" or "students with emotional and behavioral problems," is intended to apply to all of these children, whether or not they are eligible for special education services. Furthermore, the language is not intended to imply that emotional disturbance, or other mental health conditions, automatically leads to behavioral problems. Similarly, our terminology also does not imply that behavioral problems are necessarily linked with or lead to emotional disturbance.

Many children with emotional disturbance suffer from what are often termed "internalizing" problems, such as depression and anxiety, which can, unfortunately, sometimes lead to their under-identification. The message of this book is that all children with emotional and behavioral challenges need support, as do the many educators, in both general and special education, who work with them. The particular special education procedures we describe are available only to those children who have been determined eligible for special education and related services under IDEA, or who are suspected of having a disability and should therefore be referred for evaluation.

At a basic level, the good news is that the 1997 Amendments to the Individuals with Disabilities Education Act (IDEA) address many classroom concerns that have arisen over the years with respect to the discipline of students with disabilities who have behavior problems (see Table 1.1). The reauthorized statute, in fact, includes provisions designed to: (1) improve services for all students with disabilities, including those with emotional disturbance and behavioral difficulties; (2) address problem behaviors; and (3) foster an effective learning environment for all students. There are also additions to IDEA that offer support to educators who see the value of taking a proactive and collaborative approach when designing successful learning experiences for students like Clark.

Table 1.1   Provisions of the 1997 Amendments to IDEA

The Individuals with Disabilities Education Act (IDEA) is a federal law that gives guidance and direction for providing educational services to students with disabilities. Originally passed in 1975 as the Education for All Handicapped Children Act, IDEA was reauthorized by Congress in 1997. Many provisions in IDEA Amendments of 1997 address and clarify procedures for improving services to students with disabilities who also have behavioral issues.

- Increased involvement by regular education teachers in planning educational programs.

- The use of a variety of supplementary supports and services and other accommodations and modifications that must be in place for children with disabilities to succeed.

- The use of functional behavioral assessments to identify the appropriate positive behavioral supports and strategies.

- Provisions for training personnel (both special and regular educators) to appropriately provide services to children with disabilities consistent with the requirements of IDEA.

This Guidebook—A Practical Place to Start

Teachers, paraprofessionals, and school psychologists (whom we sometimes refer to collectively as educators) are on the front lines when it comes to ensuring that students with emotional and behavioral problems are given every opportunity to learn. Hence, this guidebook was designed to provide educators with a place to start—a base of practical knowledge for helping students build a successful education experience.

Many of the strategies educators find most successful do a great deal to improve the classroom experience for all students. For that reason, this book contains general strategies as well as specialized approaches, and it answers questions often asked by classroom practitioners who must address the learning and behavioral needs of all students. These strategies and techniques, used successfully in real classrooms, are offered as examples for practitioners to consider. Also included are strategies and approaches that reflect the guidelines set out in the *National Agenda for Achieving Better Results for Children and Youth with Serious Emotional Disturbance,* developed and published by the U.S. Department of Education, Office of Special Education Programs (OSEP) with assistance from the American Institutes for Research (AIR)(1994). Examples used throughout the book were gathered from schools across the country that embrace the spirit and intent of the principles espoused in the *National Agenda* (Table 1.2 summarizes the individual goals of the *National Agenda*).

This resource is predicated on a "strengths-based approach" that considers the "whole child." The instructional practices presented reflect the understanding that all students have strengths that can provide a foundation for curriculum planning, instructional programming, and classroom management. Effective teaching makes use of students' strengths, builds instructional programs that capitalize on what students are able to achieve, and helps students meet high academic standards and high standards of conduct.

Table 1.2   National Agenda for Achieving Better Results for Children and Youth with Serious Emotional Disturbance

Target 1: Expand Positive Learning Opportunities and Results

To foster the provision of engaging, useful, and positive learning opportunities. These opportunities should be result-driven and should acknowledge as well as respond to the experiences and needs of children and youth with serious emotional disturbance.*

Target 2: Strengthen School and Community Capacity

To foster initiatives that strengthen the capacity of schools and communities to serve students with serious emotional disturbance in the least restrictive environments appropriate.

Target 3: Value and Address Diversity

To encourage culturally competent and linguistically appropriate exchanges and collaborations among families, professionals, students, and communities. These collaborations should foster equitable outcomes for all students and result in the identification and provision of services that are responsive to issues of race, culture, gender, and social and economic status.

Target 4: Collaborate with Families

To foster collaborations that fully include family members on the team of service providers that implements family focused services to improve educational outcomes. Services should be open, helpful, culturally competent, accessible to families, and school—as well as community-based.

Target 5: Promote Appropriate Assessment

To promote practices ensuring that assessment is integral to the identification, design, and delivery of services for children and youth with SED. These practices should be culturally appropriate, ethical, and functional.

Target 6: Provide Ongoing Skill Development and Support

To foster the enhancement of knowledge, understanding, and sensitivity among all who work with children and youth with and at risk of developing serious emotional disturbance. Support and development should be ongoing and aim at strengthening the capacity of families, teachers, service providers, and other stakeholders to collaborate, persevere, and improve outcomes for children and youth with SED.

Target 7: Create Comprehensive and Collaborative Systems

To promote systems change resulting in the development of coherent services built around the individual needs of children and youth with and at risk of developing serious emotional disturbance. These services should be family-centered, community-based, and appropriately funded.

* Note: As a result of changes in the 1997 Amendments to IDEA, "serious emotional disturbance" is now more simply termed "emotional disturbance" in the regulations implementing the law.

Copies of the complete *National Agenda* with full descriptions of each target may be obtained by writing to the Center for Effective Collaboration and Practice, American Institutes for Research, 1000 Thomas Jefferson Street, Suite 400, Washington, DC 20007; by e-mailing a request to *center@air.org;* or by visiting the website at *www.air.org/cecp/resources/ntlagend.html.*

Research funded by OSEP suggests that schools consider a three-tiered prevention model for addressing the behavior of all students:

1. Schoolwide primary prevention efforts to teach expected behaviors to all students.

2. Early interventions directed at students who are at risk of developing emotional disturbance or behavioral problems.

3. More intensive services targeted at students with emotional disturbance or more serious behavioral problems.

Table 1.3 outlines the characteristics of schools that successfully employ this model.

Table 1.3 Characteristics of Schools That Successfully Employ Primary Prevention Strategies
• Expression of the value of all members of the school community.
• School environments marked by high academic expectations and clear, positive behavioral expectations.
• Student-centered instruction.
• Positive and proactive approaches to school discipline.
• Collaboration with family, community, and other service providers.
• Support for students, teachers, staff, and families that enables them to help students meet expectations.

Classroom teachers, paraprofessionals, school psychologists, and other school personnel play important roles in developing and implementing strategies that embrace these characteristics.

To ensure that this guidebook addresses the information needs of educators who work with students with emotional or behavioral problems, we consulted and engaged with teachers and paraprofessionals—both special and regular education—school psychologists, and other school personnel throughout the writing process. We are grateful for the willingness of practitioners to share their experiences with us of "what works."

The remainder of the book is organized as follows:

Chapter 2: Building a Knowledge Base. There are obvious advantages to sharing knowledge on issues related to educating students with emotional and behavioral difficulties. Chapter 2 contains basic information to help build a knowledge base and to help provide an enhanced understanding of the topic.

Chapter 3: Fostering Positive Learning Opportunities. This chapter contains strategies for structuring curriculum and instruction so that they have the most positive impact possible on student performance.

Chapter 4: Instituting a Sound Classroom Management System. Students learn best when there is order in their learning environment and they feel at ease. Chapter 4 offers tips and ideas for strengthening classroom management practices. It also describes techniques to help educators interact with students in a manner that creates a positive and supportive classroom environment.

Chapter 5: School-Based Supports. Because the success of instructional and classroom management programs can be enhanced by colleagues, families, and others, this chapter describes promising practices that many schools and districts now use to support classroom teachers and other instructional staff.

Chapter 6: Support and Resources. For readers who want to know more or who need additional help, Chapter 6 lists supplementary sources and contact information for organizations that may be of assistance.

Chapter 2

Building a
KNOWLEDGE BASE

Ms. Adams, a new first grade teacher, was completely frustrated with James. Up until now, he had been a star student; he sat at his desk, completed his work, and performed well in class. He was friendly and helpful, and he got along well with other students. But recently, all that had changed. Now he was contentious and highly distractible, and the smallest annoyance could provoke a huge outburst. He had even been sent to the principal's office on two occasions. His friends were beginning to shun him and make fun of his behavior. His academic performance had become erratic. He was beginning to keep company with some very aggressive children. Ms. Adams had tried talking with James about these changes, but he would shed no light on the subject.

Ms. Adams spoke to the counselor, Mr. Johnson, who suggested a discussion with the parents. His office made the contact, and James' mother took some time off from work to come to school. She was clearly harried and upset. When Mr. Johnson and Ms. Adams talked with her, it became clear what James' problem was. His mother and father had suddenly separated, and neither of them knew what was going to happen next. James' life had suddenly become very unpredictable. His mother said that he was "trying to be good" at home, and she had no idea that James' behavior was so unacceptable at school.

James' mother agreed to talk with James about the family situation and to let him know that his behavior had to improve in school. She also agreed to stay in touch with the school to see if his behavior was improving. The counselor offered to contact some family counselors whose fees were reasonable. The teacher said that she would document some observations about James' behavior during the day, and that she and the counselor would develop a plan of positive behavioral supports. They agreed to talk on the phone in a week (so that James' mother wouldn't have to be absent from work again) about the behavioral plan so James' mother could support the interventions at home. At that time, the counselor would provide her with the phone numbers of several family counselors.

Now that she had more information, Ms. Adams felt that she could make some sense of James' behavior and begin to help him behave more acceptably in school.

Understanding the nature of students' emotional and behavioral problems assists teachers and paraprofessionals in planning instructional programs that better meet students' needs. Working on teams and in collaborative partnerships means that all members must share a basic understanding of the characteristics and educational challenges confronting these students.

This chapter answers questions frequently asked by teachers and paraprofessionals about educating students with emotional and behavioral challenges.

Children With Emotional and Behavioral Problems

Students with emotional and behavioral problems exhibit a wide range of characteristics. The intensity of the disorder varies, as does the manner in which a disability or problem presents itself. While some students have mood disorders, such as depression, others may experience intense feelings of anger or frustration. Further, individual students react to feelings of depression, anger, or frustration in very different ways. For example, some students internalize these feelings, acting shy and withdrawn, while others may externalize their feelings, becoming violent or aggressive toward others.

School-based, multidisciplinary teams identify some students as having "emotional disturbance"—one of the disability classifications recognized under IDEA. Although state definitions and terminology may vary, the federal definition targets students who exhibit some or all of the factors described in Table 2.1 over a long period of time and, to a marked degree, that adversely affect a child's educational performance. "The term [emotional disturbance] includes schizophrenia. The term does not apply to students who are socially maladjusted, unless it is determined that they have an emotional disturbance" (IDEA Regulations 34 CFR §300.7[c][4]).

Table 2.1   Factors That Contribute to the Federal Definition of Emotional Disturbance

- An inability to learn that cannot be explained by intellectual, sensory, or health factors.

- An inability to build or maintain satisfactory interpersonal relationships with peers and teachers.

- Inappropriate types of behavior or feelings under normal circumstances.

- A general, pervasive mood of unhappiness or depression.

- A tendency to develop physical symptoms or fears associated with personal or school problems.

(34 CFR §300.7[c][4])

It is believed that students with emotional disturbance who are currently eligible to receive special education services represent only a small portion of the students with mental health needs. While most mental health experts estimate that three to eight percent of all school-age children and youth have emotional or behavioral disorders severe enough to require treatment, less than one percent (in 1996 and 1997) were identified by schools as having emotional disturbance. Contact the Center for Effective Collaboration and Practice (see Chapter 6) to access additional information on prevalence rates.

Causes of Emotional and Behavioral Problems

Professionals in the field of emotional and behavioral problems use various approaches to explain the causes. Knowledge about factors associated with emotional and behavioral problems can assist schools, teachers, and paraprofessionals in understanding how such factors actually affect student performance. Table 2.2 describes contributing factors to emotional and behavioral problems.

Table 2.2   Contributing Factors to Emotional and Behavioral Problems

1. **Biological factors.** Certain biological conditions have been associated with emotional and behavioral problems, as there appear to be genetic links to depression and schizophrenia, as well as to nutritional deficits, certain physical illnesses and injuries, and some neurological conditions.

2. **Family factors.** The environment in which children live can either help or hurt healthy development, just as a child's behavior may have both negative and positive influences upon other family members. Certain elements, too, within a child's family may increase his or her risk for developing emotional or behavioral problems. (Physical abuse, child neglect, sexual abuse, and emotional maltreatment have all been associated with "troubling behaviors" in children.)

3. **School factors.** Generally, students with emotional and behavioral problems tend to "underachieve" in school. Learning problems put them at a disadvantage in any school environment, particularly since many of these students have not developed adequate social skills by the time they enter school, and poor social skills may result in social rejection by both peers and teachers. This rejection leads to further disinterest in school and even greater underachievement and failure.

4. **Community factors.** Children are often exposed to stressors within their communities. Exposure to crime and gang violence has often been linked to a tendency to behave in ways associated with emotional and behavioral problems.

Teachers and paraprofessionals can frequently use their knowledge of these factors to evaluate and improve a student's educational experience. For instance, if it is suspected that a child's problem behavior is related to a biological factor, the child should not be "penalized" for what he or she cannot control; or, if a student's hyperactivity and distractibility are related to a neurological condition, activities requiring sustained attention should be modified and attempts made to expand the child's capacity for concentration.

The Educator's Role in Identifying and Referring Students

School personnel, especially teachers and paraprofessionals, serve a critical role in referral, diagnosis, and program planning. In fact, it is often the classroom teacher, and sometimes the paraprofessional, who begin the process of getting help for a student.

Identifying Behavior That Is Interfering With Learning

Teachers and paraprofessionals are often the first ones to recognize students' lack of success with assignments or continuous problems with their peer or adult relationships. While such factors may eventually result in a formal referral, a teacher's primary goal is to *identify interfering behaviors and to help students overcome them.* Teachers and paraprofessionals begin this process by analyzing the kinds of behavior that put students at risk.

While some emotional and behavioral problems lend themselves to relatively simple classroom interventions, others may require adjusting the child's entire instructional program. When the latter is necessary, the teacher's first point of inquiry is with others who know the child well. It is a good idea to consult with administrators, school psychologists, social workers, school counselors, other staff, and family members whenever problems disrupt teaching and learning. In addition, a growing number of schools have formed "assistance teams" that offer help in validating observations and recommending interventions; however, this strategy cannot be used to delay an appropriate referral of a child suspected of having a disability. Families can usually provide insight regarding their children's strengths, special needs, and stressful situations they may be experiencing in their daily lives.

Over the last few decades, many districts have established "prereferral systems"—the goal of which is to serve the student's and teacher's needs *before* a more formal approach is undertaken. Again, however, these systems cannot be used to delay appropriate referral of a child suspected of having a disability. Within prereferral systems, teachers seek help in working with a child who has presented significant and recurring problems. As part of the assistance process, teachers and paraprofessionals are frequently asked to document the "presenting problem," along with the different strategies that have been used to ameliorate it. Colleagues then review such information with the teacher and make suggestions.

The Referral Process

In the event that preventive interventions are not working and collegial help has run its course, it may be necessary to initiate a formal referral. When school officials begin to suspect that a child's behavior may indicate a disability, the child must be referred for appropriate evaluation. A teacher's role at the referral stage is not to make a diagnosis but to work as part of the team that develops and implements a formal evaluation. Teachers will likely be asked to present concrete information describing the student's behavior, the situations in which that behavior occurs, and any interventions that have already been tried. Any documentation that the teacher, paraprofessional, or other school staff has made will be helpful in this process.

As part of the referral process, teachers are sometimes asked to provide additional documentation of the student's behavior, focusing on particular details. Such a practice is helpful, as it reveals characteristics that ultimately may result in a more effective behavioral intervention plan. In considering a student's behavior, it is important to use a "strengths-based approach," which means that in addition to identifying challenging behaviors, positive learning behaviors and other student strengths also are identified (see Table 2.3). It is valuable to *specify* strengths; that is, to identify instances when the child is engaged or well behaved.

▬▬▬ Documenting Behaviors

Generally, the first step in identifying behaviors is to define the behavior being measured in concrete and observable terms. Defining behavior as "disruptive" or "dangerous" does not *specify* the behavior; therefore, it will not be helpful when planning interventions. Better definitions might be "loud yelling in the classroom," "pushing a classmate," or "tapping a pencil continuously"—behaviors that can be objectively observed and measured.

**Table 2.3   Questions That May Help Guide a
Strengths-Based Assessment**

1. **Are there any recurrent behavior patterns?** For example, the teacher may note that the behavior does not occur all day, but only during activities in which the student must read and comprehend information.

2. **Under what conditions is the student most successful?** For example, the student may do well in highly structured tasks where the expectations and directions are clearly articulated.

3. **What conditions tend to trigger the problem behavior?** For example, after recording outbursts for a week, the paraprofessional finds that most problem behavior occurs when the student is asked to work with other classmates.

4. **What tends to hold the student's attention?** For example, a teacher may discover that a student *can* concentrate for more than 30 minutes when engaged in manipulative mathematics tasks.

Several observational strategies are typically used in school settings to document behavior (see Table 2.4). In some cases, multiple techniques are more helpful in understanding a student's behavior patterns.

Table 2.4   Common Observational Strategies

1. **Identifying patterns.** This technique is used to identify possible patterns of behavior by pinpointing the specific events that precede (also called antecedents) or follow (also called consequences) the problem behavior that may serve to maintain it. Observers keep a written record of everything they see and hear and note the entire context in which the target behavior occurs during the documentation time periods. Observation narratives are most useful when they are completed in several settings over different periods of time.

2. **Measuring frequency.** This strategy is used to measure the number of times a behavior occurs during a designated period. The teacher defines the behavior, observes the student at specified times, and notes how often the behavior occurs (e.g., the number of times a student uses profanity during a class lecture).

3. **Measuring duration.** This technique is used to measure the length of time a student engages in the particular behavior of interest (e.g., the amount of time a student engages in daydreaming behavior during math activities).

Although recording strategies are associated with referral, many teachers find that classroom-based observational data can uncover the source of many problems and lead to their correction. An educator may discover, for instance, that a student swears only when in the presence of *certain* peers. Or, in some cases, the student's behavior may be shown to be a response—albeit, inappropriate—to the provocations of others. Data, in brief, provide educators with new avenues to explore in addressing students' behavioral needs.

Careful evaluation of children suspected of being emotionally disturbed generally involves an assessment of their behavior if the behavior interferes with their learning or the learning of others. Districts and states should have procedures in place for student evaluation and assessment that ensure compliance with the 1997 amendments to IDEA and with Section 504 of the Rehabilitation Act of 1973. Once such procedures are established, the evaluation of students with emotional disturbance should be *multifaceted, culturally nonbiased,* and generally include:

- Classroom observations by evaluators

- Results of all interventions (i.e., teacher documentation and team information)

- Interviews, checklists, and questionnaires completed by teachers, family members, and the child, as appropriate, including developmental, health, and sensory data

- Psychological or psychiatric evaluations

- Previous academic evaluations, including work samples

- A review of the child's school history

Because of their direct experience, classroom teachers often are called upon by the evaluation team to complete assessment tasks and to share what they know about a student. Information gained from experience, after all, is invaluable to interpret student behavior and to craft a successful intervention.

Considering Cultural Differences

It is important to remember that everyone's behavior is influenced by his or her culture and subcultures (e.g., geographical region, neighborhood, religious beliefs, age, or gender). When educators become concerned about a child's behavior, they must make a determination as to whether the behavior is the result of a cultural difference rather than a behavioral deficit. In some cases, behaviors merely reflect the student's cultural background, which differs from that of the educator or school system.

Educators should discuss with students and their family members behaviors that may be influenced by culture. For example, some Native American cultures frown on competition, so children will not give answers in class that might make them appear smarter than their classmates. The educators and family members together should then decide whether a replacement behavior should be taught (e.g., teaching the child to be competitive); if the child should be taught to use different behaviors in different situations (e.g., teaching the child that competition is appropriate under certain circumstances); or if the school should make accommodations to respect the child's cultural differences (e.g., use cooperative learning rather than competitive techniques). In any case, educators need to be cognizant of how their own cultural beliefs influence their behavior as well as how they perceive the behavior of others.

▬▬▬▬ Working With Students Who Have Been Identified as Needing Support

Students often begin attending a school having been identified as qualifying for specially designed instruction or services under IDEA. Still, even though students may already be receiving special education and related services, teachers and paraprofessionals have the major responsibility for educating them.

Even today, many questions remain about where students with emotional disturbance are to receive their education. Federal regulations, however, are clear, and specify that "to the maximum extent appropriate, children with disabilities, including children in public or private institutions or other care facilities, are educated with children who are non-disabled" (34 CFR §300.550[b][1]). This requirement does not mandate that students be served in regular school environments if such placements are inappropriate. In fact, federal regulations mandate that each public agency ensure that "a continuum of alternative placements is available to meet the needs of children with disabilities for special education and related services" (34 CFR §300.551[a]), and that "supplementary services (such as resource room or intinerant instruction), . . . be provided in conjunction with regular class placement" (34 CFR §300.551[b][2]).

Nevertheless, removal of children with disabilities from the regular educational environment—including removal to special classes or separate schools—must occur "only if the nature or severity of the disability is such that education in regular classes with the use of supplementary aids and services cannot be achieved satisfactorily" (34 CFR §300.550[b][2]).

In addition, IDEA '97 states that "school personnel may order a change in placement of a child with a disability to an appropriate interim, alternative educational setting for the same amount of time that a child without a disability would be subject to discipline, but for not more than 45 days if (i) the child carries a weapon to school or to a school function . . . or (ii) the child knowingly possesses or uses illegal drugs or sells or solicits the sale of a controlled substance while at school or a school function . . ." (34 CFR §300.520[a][2]).

Under the IDEA amendments, a hearing officer may also order a change in the placement of a child with a disability to an interim, alternative educational setting for not more than 45 days under very explicit conditions. These conditions are spelled out in Sec. 615(k)(2) of the statute and in 34 CFR §300.521 of the regulations. The statutory language may be found in Appendix A on pages 72 and 73. Appendix A contains all of the statutory language that pertains to students with disabilities who have behavioral problems.

In general, when making placement decisions, the group making the decision about placement must give consideration to the full range of supplementary supports and services that could be provided to accommodate the needs of individual students with disabilities.

If it is decided that the least restrictive environment (LRE) for a child is the regular classroom, the child's teacher should be informed about the child's strengths and needs as well as any information helpful in planning an instructional program. Similarly, because the student's regular classroom teacher will be responsible for implementing the student's individualized education program (IEP), IDEA regulations require the local education agency to ensure that "the child's

IEP is accessible to each regular . . . [and] special education teacher, related service provider, and other service provider who is responsible for its implementation" (34 CFR §300.342[b][2]). In addition, each teacher and provider must be informed of "his or her specific responsibilities related to implementing the child's IEP; and the specific accommodations, modifications, and supports that must be provided for the child in accordance with the IEP" (34 CFR §300.342[b][3]).

If a child is or may be participating in the regular classroom environment, at least one of the child's regular education teachers must be a member of the child's IEP team. In fact, once an IEP is completed, it is the classroom teacher who is often responsible for monitoring the student's achievement, with the help of other members of the team. Classroom teachers and paraprofessionals should express their concerns to the IEP team and the administration when necessary, and, in order to be successful, teachers must have sufficient support from the team and the administration to implement IEPs.

When a student with a disability exhibits behaviors that interfere with his or her learning or the learning of others, the IEP team must consider, if appropriate, strategies that include positive behavioral interventions, strategies, and supports to address those behaviors. These strategies and supports (1) should be based on a functional behavioral assessment, (2) should establish clear expectations about appropriate behavior, (3) and should be designed to help the student succeed. The team monitors the student's behavior regularly, and if it is not satisfactory, the team modifies the strategies and supports.

What Educators Need to Know About Students Taking Medication

Because some students are on a regimen of prescription medication, teachers and paraprofessionals should acquire a working knowledge of this treatment intervention. Table 2.5 lists prescription drugs used to treat students with emotional and behavioral problems. Qualified medical professionals prescribe medication, and qualified nursing professionals should help administer and monitor a student's medication. Educators, however, can and do have a valuable role and a vested interest in their students' medical treatment. Educators can:

- *Make certain that students receive medication on schedule.* Generally, this means reminding students to go to the nurse's office to take their medicine.

- *Observe students' behavior and note instances that support the use of medication or suggest the presence of medication side effects.* If possible side effects occur, a teacher or other school staff member should notify the school nurse or other appropriate school personnel and/or the family. If necessary, the teacher should seek help. Appropriate personnel (e.g., a psychologist and/or nurse) should be available to assist with evaluating the effects of medication on students' learning.

The use of a medication to address behavior assumes some behaviors that interfere with learning and classroom participation can be chemically controlled. Central nervous system stimulants, for example, are sometimes used to treat children with attention deficit hyperactivity disorder (ADHD). When working properly, these stimulants can temporarily reduce the symptoms of

Table 2.5   Prescription Medications Used to Treat Students
With Emotional Difficulties

- Stimulants are used to focus attention and energy while decreasing impulsive behaviors. Examples are Cylert, Ritalin, Dexedrine, and Benzedrine.

- Tranquilizers help suppress hyperactivity, aggressiveness, self-injurious behaviors, and hallucinations. Examples are Thorazine, Mellaril, and Haldol.

- Antidepressants are prescribed to alter moods, reduce hyperactivity and aggression, and to treat school phobias. Examples are Tofranil, Prozac, and Elavil.

- Anticonvulsants are used to control seizures and convulsions. Examples are phenobarbital, Mysoline, Dilantin, and Valium.

hyperactivity and impulsivity and increase concentration. However, even when medication works properly, other interventions, including sound educational instruction and positive behavioral supports, are still needed to ensure success.

Possible drug side effects represent major treatment drawbacks. When working with a student on medication, it is important to be aware of the side effects associated with the drug, as such awareness will aid in recognition of which behavior(s) the student cannot control. Furthermore, such knowledge will enable educators to alert other educators, school officials, and family members should the student demonstrate behaviors associated with recognizable side effects. Two good resources regarding medication side effects are *Medications for Children with Behavior and Emotional Problems: A Primer for Parents* (Hutchens, Canter, and Carroll 1998) and *Medical Management of Behavior and Emotional Problems in Children and Adolescents: A Primer for Educators* (Carroll 1998). To obtain a copy of either or both of these publications, educators can ask their school psychologist or contact the National Association of School Psychologists (NASP) (see Chapter 6).

Getting Support From Others

Across the country, families, school psychologists, mental health specialists, and other special service providers are beginning to work with teachers and paraprofessionals to foster cooperative and positive learning opportunities for students with emotional and behavioral problems. Building collaborative partnerships is, in fact, a key ingredient in supporting these students, both in regular education classrooms and in other environments.

Many schools already have teacher support teams, prereferral teams, or child study teams that offer suggestions for remediating classroom dilemmas. Many special educators, behavior specialists, and school psychologists are well versed in emotional and behavioral strategies and, thus, may be invaluable sources of ideas and information. Properly trained and supervised paraprofessionals can also be instrumental in implementing small-group and individual behavioral interventions, and administrators can be consulted for recommendations and resources. Other professionals might be available to assist the teacher or student, either on a permanent or an as-needed basis.

Special education teachers, paraprofessionals, school social workers, and school psychologists all can develop many of the skills necessary to support students with emotional disturbance. Additional interventions, which are sometimes identified in the student's IEP, are often provided by a variety of support specialists (see Table 2.6). Understanding the different functions that support service personnel perform can help teachers take advantage of all available resources.

Table 2.6   Typical Functions of Support Specialists
• Counseling (psychiatrist/psychologist)
• Behavioral and therapeutic management (behavior specialist)
• Liaison between the school, the child, family members, and community agencies (social services facilitator or case manager)
• Coordination of services for students currently involved with the juvenile justice system (juvenile justice caseworker)

Educators also can learn about students with emotional and behavioral problems from students' families. The family is, after all, the most obvious source of information about a student's behavior. As defined here, a "family" extends beyond the birth, adoptive, or foster parents to include all adults who influence the day-to-day care of the student as well as other members of the family unit. In some families, grandparents, aunts, or uncles serve in primary care roles. Including families in the child's education program can enhance its relevance and chance for success.

Educators who have formed partnerships with other professionals and family members have discovered effective ways to serve the educational needs of students with emotional and behavioral problems while, at the same time, expanding their repertoire of successful strategies appropriate for all students. However, given the scheduling constraints in many schools, collaboration often requires creative juggling of time. Sometimes it is best to include the estimated time needed to complete the tasks involved (e.g., how long a discussion will last or how long an observation will take) when initiating a request for support.

Some ways to access information and support include:

• Finding out if the school offers teacher support or assistance teams.

• Contacting available support personnel and meeting with them on a regular basis.

• Asking administrators to provide classroom release time so that educators can attend relevant meetings.

Some students have needs that transcend the classroom, as well as the time and capabilities of classroom teachers. In such cases, intensive services should be brought to bear to assist the student. The group making placement decisions needs to consider the full continuum of services and placements, as described in IDEA regulations (see Table 2.7).

Table 2.7   IDEA Continuum of Alternative Placements

(a) Each public agency shall ensure that a continuum of alternative placements is available to meet the needs of children with disabilities for special education and related services.

(b) The continuum required in paragraph (a) of this section must—

   (1) Include the alternative placements listed in the definition of special education under §300.26 (instruction in regular classes, special classes, special schools, home instruction, and instruction in hospitals and institutions); and

   (2) Make provision for supplementary services (such as resource room or itinerant instruction) to be provided in conjunction with regular class placement.

(34 CFR §300.551)

Moving Forward

When teachers and paraprofessionals understand the nature of their students' emotional and behavioral problems, instructional programs have a much better chance of producing academic results. Basic knowledge concerning identification and diagnosis can go a long way in broadening perspective. Most teachers will seek to apply this knowledge directly to the classroom, quite simply because teaching informed by the research on quality instruction is perhaps the best intervention. Some approaches are worth considering, however, as they have proven to enhance the classroom learning of students with emotional and behavioral problems. The next chapter describes some of those approaches.

Chapter 3

Fostering Positive
LEARNING OPPORTUNITIES

Ms. Dunlap, the special education teacher, and Mr. Frieze, the sixth grade teacher, decided to combine their classes for an interdisciplinary unit. They began by making a list of basic academic skills their students needed, then they developed a list of social skills necessary to participate successfully in learning activities.

Realizing that some students had not mastered all the required social skills, the teachers divided the class period into segments. During the first segment, students received instruction in the social skills needed for the day's lesson. In the next segment, the students applied the skills in a hands-on, inquiry-based learning activity. During the final segment, students worked independently on their culminating projects, and, at the end of the period, students rated their own academic and social skills performance.

Effective instructional strategies assume that educators take into account the strengths and needs of their students when designing any lesson. Like their classmates, *students with emotional and behavioral problems learn best in classrooms characterized by effective instruction and behavior management routines.* As educators know, students benefit most when academic tasks and instructional strategies are carefully designed to engage them and support their learning, and when expectations and rules are clearly communicated to them.

When working in the classroom with students with emotional or behavioral challenges, it is important to remember that when the curriculum and instructional strategies do not capitalize on the students' strengths and address learning needs, frustration may result in the form of acting-out or withdrawn behaviors. The challenge is to minimize such counterproductive experiences while simultaneously providing positive learning opportunities.

Designing successful opportunities for students with emotional and behavioral challenges may require educators to change how they plan and organize their instruction, manage their classrooms, and arrange the physical layout of the classroom. These additional efforts will not only benefit students with emotional and behavior difficulties, they will likely help all students realize greater success.

Promoting Academic Success

Like all children, students with emotional and behavioral problems vary in their characteristics and needs, in their likes and dislikes, and in their reactions to classroom events. A student's cultural background also may affect how he or she reacts to certain academic situations. While there are many ways to modify a lesson in order to accommodate all students, a good place to

This chapter explores how teachers can structure curriculum and instruction that have a positive impact upon student performance.

start is with those aspects of the learning setting that pose the most challenges, such as task difficulty, lesson presentation, motivational strategies, and work assignments.

The following strategies can be used to benefit the learning of all students, not merely those with emotional and behavioral challenges. Also, because no two classrooms are alike, it is assumed that teachers and other professionals will use their own expert judgment regarding whether a particular strategy may or may not be useful in their own settings.

Task Difficulty

Teachers usually review curriculum materials before planning instruction. They have discovered, through experience, that most students avoid tasks *if* they believe they will fail. Therefore, it is important to ensure that students are not only challenged, but that they are capable of succeeding. Fear of failure is particularly relevant when dealing with students with emotional and behavioral problems, as so many have a history of failure. The problems that such students experience in school often lead to gaps in their skill levels, or "splinter skills," that make schoolwork even more difficult.

One strategy helpful in building opportunities for success is targeting the necessary skills the student may need to improve upon. For example, directions may be written at a sixth grade level, but a student may have only third grade reading skills. Vigorous attempts must be made to try to bring the student's reading skills up to grade level, and, until that happens, modifications should be made that prevent the student from experiencing difficulty in reading the assignment directions. The key is to predict, modify, or avoid situations in which the student may encounter problems. This procedure, referred to as "precorrection," will help the student meet challenges and cope with problems.

Predicting where students may have difficulty permits educators to *build in* instructional supports. One area in which students with emotional and behavioral problems struggle is working in small groups. Social skills—listening, waiting one's turn, asking questions, taking responsibility, interrupting appropriately, dealing with mistakes—are skills that students need to possess in order to succeed in group interactions. Because many students with emotional or behavioral challenges have not mastered these social skills, and because students from diverse cultures may have learned different group interaction skills, they may require additional support or training *before* they are able to participate fully in group activities. Table 3.1 suggests ways to maintain student engagement during lessons.

Lesson Presentation

When students are actively engaged in learning, they are less likely to misbehave. Teachers and paraprofessionals can increase engagement by incorporating the principles of effective instruction into their lessons (e.g., efficient classroom management, students given frequent opportunities to respond, students challenged by work but not defeated by it). Specific suggestions for increasing student engagement appear in Table 3.2.

Planning short review lessons or readiness activities can help orient the student to a particular learning task. Whenever possible, it is also important to build on students' experiences when

Table 3.1   Maintaining Student Engagement

- Keep lesson objectives clear.
- Deliver lessons in a lively manner and make sure students are engaged.
- Use concrete vocabulary and clear, succinct sentences.
- Model cognitive strategies, such as "thinking aloud," that encourage students to verbalize the thought processes required by the task.
- Give all students immediate encouragement and specific feedback.
- Use meaningful materials and manipulatives and provide examples that students can relate to.
- Have students recite in unison.
- Vary tone of voice and model enthusiasm.
- Prompt students to answer questions, after allowing an appropriate amount of "wait time," to encourage participation (this may vary depending on the child's cultural background).
- Avoid digressions as much as is possible.
- Use interesting visual and auditory presentations to entice students to attend to tasks.

Table 3.2   Suggestions for Increasing Academic Engagement Time

1. **Break long presentations into shorter segments.** At the end of each segment, have students respond in some way.

2. **Extend the amount of time students are given to complete particular tasks.**

3. **Break down assignments into smaller ones.** As students finish each mini-assignment, build in reinforcements for task completion. Wait to distribute the next assignment until students have been successful with the current one.

4. **Reduce the number of practice items** that a student must complete, once the student has demonstrated mastery.

5. **When students make mistakes, help them learn from those mistakes.** Be careful not to "overcorrect," or require compensation beyond the point where the student can demonstrate mastery, and praise any progress toward the desired behavior change.

6. **Follow low-interest activities with high-interest activities** so that students get breaks between difficult activities and those that are less challenging.

presenting new information. This helps everyone see the value of learning new skills. Students who learn to share their experiences with their classmates are able to learn from and about one another. This, in turn, can enhance their ability to form positive peer relationships.

If students have difficulty staying engaged in a lesson, modifications can be made. For example, to accommodate the learning characteristics of a short attention span, some teachers vary the length of the material presented. Holding students' interest and attention can be challenging under the best conditions; therefore, it is wise to experiment and ask colleagues for ideas and suggestions.

Motivational Strategies

The key to motivation is to increase student participation in learning activities. With the proper incentives, sometimes called "reinforcers," even students who show little interest can be coaxed into performing. Incentives need not be restricted to tangible reinforcers, such as points that can be traded in for rewards, stickers, food, etc. Many teachers successfully rely more on social, intangible incentives/reinforcers like content that is related to students' interests and lives, social praise, positive and corrective feedback, his or her own enthusiasm, or presentations that capture student interest.

Table 3.3 lists other strategies teachers can employ, which have particular application to students with emotional and behavioral challenges, to make their lessons interesting, relevant, and motivating.

Table 3.3   Strategies for Increasing Student Motivation
1. **Build upon student interests.** Students often learn by relating material to real-life situations that they find interesting. Building interest into projects, activities, and illustrative examples is important for increasing students' motivation.
2. **Allow students to make choices.** Let students decide between two tasks or select the order in which they complete assigned tasks.
3. **Use age-appropriate materials and activities.** Students often balk at performing tasks they perceive to be geared toward students younger than themselves.
4. **Vary activities and the pace at which those activities are presented** so that students can maintain interest and focus. When working with students with language difficulties, alternate activities that require writing skills (e.g., describing a single-celled organism) with those that require other modes of responding and learning (e.g., diagramming a single-celled organism) to help students sustain involvement.
5. **Employ appropriate technology applications** (e.g., computer-assisted instruction programs, CD-ROM demonstrations, videotape presentations) that can engage student interest and increase motivation.
6. **Use hands-on, experiential learning activities** to enable students to apply learning to the real world. This is one of a teacher's most powerful tools.

In addition to infusing motivational techniques into lessons, teachers can celebrate student progress by building a means to recognize and encourage not only participation, but intellectual accomplishments as well (see Table 3.4).

Whenever tangible forms of recognition are paired with social reinforcement, such as social praise and positive and corrective feedback, it is important to explain exactly what students have

Table 3.4   Ways to Recognize and Encourage Students

- **Awards:** Use certificates or symbolic objects as awards for task completion.

- **Bonus points:** Some students benefit from working toward a tangible goal on an hourly, daily, or weekly basis. With a bonus points system, students earn points that can be saved up and cashed in later for a reward. When designing a points system for students with emotional and behavioral challenges, it is important to design tasks and time frames that fit the students. For example, if the payoff is too far into the future, the student may give up on the task.

- **Accomplishment sheets:** Have students record their progress on a chart or record sheet that enables them to see their progression toward a goal.

- **Personal notes:** Some students like to receive notes from teachers or paraprofessionals. Such notes provide encouragement to both the student and his or her family.

- **Novel rewards:** The process by which a student acquires a reward can be motivating in itself, if it is age appropriate. Dot-to-dot drawings can be used to collect points, with the student earning the right to connect the dots by accomplishing specified tasks. Or, give students shapes that represent pizza ingredients; once the "dough" is covered, they earn a pizza party.

accomplished and how those accomplishments will help them achieve long-term goals in school and in the world outside of school. At the same time, keep in mind that some students (particularly shy students or some teenagers) prefer to keep their rewards private, especially when they are praised for their behavioral progress.

Work Assignments

Many students with emotional and behavioral difficulties need special help learning "how to learn," as they lack the study or organizational skills that would enable them to work independently at tasks over a sustained period of time. Table 3.5 describes strategies for fostering these skills.

Involving Others

There is much that educators can do to foster positive learning experiences, and there is a great deal that other professionals and those knowledgeable about the student can contribute as well. For instance, if the student is receiving some form of therapeutic support, it is almost always a good idea for the therapist to regularly solicit input from other service providers, such as the classroom teacher or the guidance counselor.

When planning new lessons, teachers have found it productive to capitalize on the insights and support that family members can provide. *Family input and support should be solicited, and families should be informed of their children's progress on a regular basis.* These points are emphasized because, too often, families are asked to participate *only* when their children are having difficulties.

Table 3.5	Strategies for Fostering Study and Organizational Skills

1. Teach students to keep track of assignments, grades, and targeted behaviors with reminders, such as assignment sheets, daily schedules, and to-do lists.

2. Highlight behavioral and academic successes with some form of daily record of work assignments and accomplishments. When collected over time, such records document student progress and become motivators for continued student effort.

3. Have students take notes from both oral presentations and textbooks in order to give them a means for sorting out and reviewing information.

4. Help students manage their time by establishing routines for making transitions between lessons, getting and putting away materials, and requesting assistance.

5. Have students put away unnecessary items in designated storage areas. Too many materials may cause distractions during work time.

6. Provide time management reminders, such as ten-, five-, or two-minute warnings before cleanup time, to establish time limitations for completing work.

7. Make sure students actually understand all directions before they begin working independently.

Sharing responsibility for the student's academic progress often results in a network of support. By sharing knowledge, expertise, and support, educators have a much better chance of reaching students with emotional and behavioral problems.

Moving Forward

The classroom practitioner's major responsibility is to provide a quality academic program for all students, including students who face emotional and behavioral challenges. Sound instructional planning goes hand in hand with effective classroom management. The next chapter describes how teachers and other instructional personnel can strengthen their behavioral management and discipline systems to support *all* students, especially those with emotional and behavioral problems.

Chapter 4

Instituting a Sound
CLASSROOM MANAGEMENT SYSTEM

At the beginning of every school year, teachers at Sherrill Street Elementary School agree on five basic rules applicable to all students, and during the first week of school, they devote time to teaching and reinforcing the five agreed-upon rules. Many teachers produce bulletin board displays in the hallways that serve as reminders of those rules. The principal supports this effort by making statements concerning the five rules in all of her opening announcements. Special service personnel also contribute by making self-control cards on which the rules are written and supplying those cards to students who need additional support in mastering the rules.

Cristina, a student at Sherrill Street Elementary, had difficulty stopping one activity and moving on to a new one. When told to stop what she was doing, Cristina usually ignored the command or began screaming "No!" Rather than just assuming that Cristina had mastered the necessary transition skills, her paraprofessional, Ms. Avery, decided to teach a transition routine to her. Once Ms. Avery was convinced that Cristina had mastered that routine, she initiated a contingency system in which Cristina earned points for appropriate behavior during transitions.

In addition, to help Cristina prepare for important, upcoming changes, Ms. Avery began cuing her five minutes in advance, a strategy that is helping Cristina make transitions with less resistance.

Although not panaceas for all behavioral problems, classroom management systems, including individual or group behavior plans that provide clear behavioral expectations and are taught and implemented on a schoolwide basis, do provide a supportive structure for students. At a minimum, by concentrating on a limited number of rules, educators provide the essential foundation for improving student behavior and promoting student success. All students, especially students with emotional and behavioral problems, need to know what is expected of them.

Teachers can enhance education for all students by establishing a sound classroom management system and by clearly articulating expectations and goals. Students may also need to have positive behavioral supports as part of their IEPs, as Cristina did. Based upon a careful assessment of the conditions associated with the student's troublesome behavior (through tools like a functional behavioral assessment), positive behavioral supports can prevent behavior problems in that they establish clear expectations about appropriate behavior and provide the supports necessary for the student to succeed.

This chapter explores how teachers and paraprofessionals can strengthen their classroom management systems to provide a positive environment and to accommodate the special needs of students with emotional and behavioral problems.

▬▬▬▬▬ System for Managing the Classroom

A sound classroom management system can provide exactly the structure students (especially those with emotional and behavioral problems) need for *managing their own behaviors*. All components of a classroom management system are important, but the most important are: (1) arranging the physical environment, (2) setting rules and expectations, (3) helping students comply with rules and expectations, (4) scheduling the day, (5) establishing routines and procedures, and (6) building a positive classroom climate that provides all students opportunities for success.

Arranging the Physical Environment

Educators can discourage challenging behavior by the way they manage space. Here are some suggestions:

- **Delineate space:** Some students intuitively read the subtle cues that define the purposes for different classroom areas and how they should behave in those areas; however, other students need to be taught how to navigate the classroom. It often helps such students to have the classroom space divided into areas that have clear purposes.

- **Control the degree of stimulation:** Teachers have significant influence over the amount of visual and auditory stimulation students receive within the classroom, and, therefore, they should be aware that students who are easily distracted may require less stimulation than is typical. Examples of relatively easy steps to accommodate such students include covering storage areas, removing unused equipment from sight, replacing a loud aquarium motor with a quiet one, and keeping classroom displays organized.

- **Monitor high-traffic areas:** There tends to be a lot of movement in areas surrounding the pencil sharpener, water faucet, wastebasket, and the teacher's desk. Students who are easily distracted should be seated away from such areas, yet still within the proximity, or at least the eyesight, of the teacher or paraprofessional. In addition, procedures for using these areas should be developed and taught.

- **Establish a quiet place:** Some students may need a quiet, "safe" place to sit and work or to calm down after an emotional outburst. Study carrels, desk blinders (three-paneled cardboard pieces that students can use at their seats for privacy), or an area behind a bookcase are examples of such quiet places. It is important to note, however, that all students should remain in full view of the teacher or paraprofessional at all times. Also, students benefit from feeling ownership of their belongings and, thus, will profit from having a personal space to store them.

Setting Rules and Expectations

At the beginning of the year, teachers typically establish rules for classroom behavior. One technique that may increase compliance with such rules is to explain them in positive, concrete terms that describe the behavior that is expected of them (e.g., raising one's hand to be called upon to talk), rather than defining what behavior is not acceptable (e.g., no talking). Similarly, consequences for failing to meet expectations should be logical, fair, predictable, directed at the inappropriate behavior, and, of course, explained before an infraction occurs. Once five or six rules have been stated clearly, it is important to teach students how to follow them.

Helping Students Comply With Rules and Expectations

Educators sometimes assume that students know how to carry out directives when, in fact, they do not know how. Students with emotional and behavioral problems are especially prone to being punished for breaking rules, even though they sometimes lack the skills necessary to follow them. If, for example, the classroom rule is to "listen when others are talking," then some students will need to be taught the skills necessary for listening.

From the beginning of their educational experience, students should know the consequences of breaking rules, and the consequences must be fair and consistently enforced. Typically, students with emotional and behavioral challenges have difficulty understanding the consequences of their behavior. If a student breaks a rule, then it is wise to ask that student to explain the consequence of his or her actions.

Consider these points when developing classroom rules:

- Rules need to be stated in clear and explicit behavioral terms; it is difficult for students to abide by rules they don't understand. For instance, what does it mean to be "responsible" or to be "nice"? Children, especially younger children, need concrete terms and examples they can understand, such as raising their hands before speaking.

- Rules must be concise in order for students to remember them. Reminders also may be posted in the learning area.

- Encourage students to suggest rules themselves, which helps create a sense of ownership and accountability; however, good research shows that this is not essential to good classroom management.

Although educators can prevent many minor behavioral infractions by ensuring that rules are clearly stated, fairly enforced, and completely understood, there are often additional issues posed by students with serious behavioral problems. These are students who, after all, may have difficulty following even the most clearly stated and fairly enforced rules. For teachers and paraprofessionals to be fair and consistent, they must know whether or not a student has the necessary skills to comply with the rules.

When all good faith efforts and best practice procedures do not produce desired results, it may be time to enlist the support of the school psychologist, behavior specialist, the IEP team, special educator, and/or other support personnel. It may be that the IEP team needs to reconvene to modify the existing behavior intervention plan or academic objectives.

Depending on the effect of the behavior on the safety and learning opportunities for the student and for other students in the classroom, the group responsible for making placements may need to consider a change of placement if concerted, documented efforts to modify serious behavior problems prove to be unsuccessful.

Scheduling the Day

For students with emotional or behavioral problems, several considerations might be useful when scheduling activities throughout the day. For instance, time for students to calm down while in a state of transition to a more structured activity can be built into the day's schedule. Also, since many students who have behavioral challenges find it difficult to maintain attention for long periods of physically inactive work time, it can be helpful to break large tasks into several smaller tasks with short breaks between them.

Establishing Routines and Procedures

Establishing routines for *how* things are done and then teaching those routines can help students stay on target in the classroom. For example, it is important to implement consistent routines for those times when students have to make a transition from one lesson to another, or for times when they have to retrieve and put away materials, and so on. Routines can, of course, be taught, and students can be rewarded for following them. Table 4.1 lists ways to support students in performing routine tasks.

Table 4.1   Tactics to Help Students Accomplish Routine Tasks

1. **Student cue cards.** Small, wallet-size cards upon which transition steps are written can serve as visual cues, which can be taped to a student's desk, written in a notebook, or carried in a pocket. The teacher or paraprofessional may, in practice, direct students' attention to the card before moving on to a transition period.

2. **Reflection time.** Many educators find that having students stop all activity for a moment and reflect upon what they are going to do next goes a long way in preparing them for an actual transition.

3. **Advance notice.** Because some students find it difficult to cognitively or emotionally disengage from an activity in which they are immersed, advance notice (such as a five-minute warning prior to the activity's end) prepares them for disengagement and movement toward the next activity.

4. **Peer support.** When a student is learning a new routine or is having difficulty following a procedure, many teachers assign a "peer buddy" to reinforce and guide the student through the required transition steps.

5. **Subtle prompts.** Pointing to a clock or putting away materials can cue students that it is time for a change. Praise or encouragement also can be used effectively to prepare for a transition. For example, saying "Ginny, you have really worked hard on your paper," or, "Look how much you have written today," helps to focus the student's attention on "wrapping up" the activity.

Building a Positive Classroom Climate That Provides All Students Opportunities for Success

Allison rarely spoke in class, and when she did, it was in a whisper. Concerned, Ms. Davis, the language arts teacher, built a rapport with her silent student. Each day, Ms. Davis initiated a conversation with Allison (as did Ms. Peters, the para-professional). Patient efforts paid off, and Allison gradually began giving more than one-word answers.

Communicating respect, in addition to setting high but attainable expectations for academic performance, is central to supporting growth in the classroom. For students with emotional and behavioral challenges, building a rapport through mutual respect and acceptance is, in fact, the first step toward establishing trust. Table 4.2 provides teacher-recommended techniques that can facilitate respectful communication.

Table 4.2   Techniques for Communicating Respect

1. **Actively listen.** Teachers need to let students know that they are being listened to. Eye contact and paraphrasing what the student says are two simple ways to demonstrate that the teacher is, indeed, listening. However, it is important to understand that in many cultures it is considered rude for children to make eye contact with adults.

2. **Use nonthreatening questions.** When students have misbehaved, questions that focus on "what" (e.g., "What went through your mind just before you kicked your shoes into the hallway?") and "how" (e.g., "How did your math book end up in the trash?") are easier to answer than those that focus on "why" (e.g., "Why did you throw your book in the trash?"). Moreover, students with a history of behavioral difficulties have learned that "why" questions often accompany disciplinary interventions and, as a result, they often react to such questions as if they are being put on the spot. Tone of voice is also important. Questions should be asked in a tone that suggests a genuine effort toward helping the student understand the misbehavior.

3. **Use open-ended questions.** For students with a history of failure, questions that have what they perceive as a "right" or "wrong" answer make them feel uncomfortable (e.g., "Did you follow all the directions during the science lab today?"). Instead, use open-ended questions, especially when engaging the student in conversation (e.g., "What did you do in science class today?").

4. **Show personal interest in the student.** It is important for students to talk about themselves. Sharing details about likes and dislikes can open the door to broader achievements in the classroom.

Once a rapport has been established, it is vital to work toward maintaining it. Oftentimes, rapport breaks down when teachers need to discipline students; therefore, a teacher should let a student know that it is his or her *behavior* that is problematic, *not* the student as an individual. Some teachers have found that "I messages" allow them to maintain rapport while addressing behavior. An I message is a statement of the behavior, followed by the *effect* the behavior had, and concludes with the direct and tangible consequences of the behavior. For example, "When you get out of your seat while I am giving directions (the behavior), you distract me and other students (the effect), which means we all have to stop what we are doing until I can get back everyone's attention (the consequence)."

Summary

Knowing how to prevent behavior problems enables educators to move away from a reactive, punitive environment toward a more proactive environment. There is much that teachers and paraprofessionals can do to establish a classroom environment that allows all students to maximize their learning potential. At a minimum, educators can provide a foundation for improving student behavior and for promoting student success by maintaining an orderly, predictable classroom.

Preventing disturbing behavior through predictable means is clearly a major ingredient in fostering any kind of success in the classroom. There are times, however, when more corrective approaches are called for. Students in the best of classrooms will lose control of their actions on occasion, some by acting out and others by withdrawing. When teachers know how to help students manage challenging behaviors, they are better equipped to help students who have emotional and behavioral problems.

▬▬▬ Managing Behavior

> Kevin, a new student in Mr. Blanchard's fifth grade class, was constantly out of his seat and completed very few assignments. During one half-hour period, Mr. Blanchard noted that Kevin sharpened his pencil five times, got three drinks of water, and went to the materials table four times. Determined to decrease Kevin's "roaming," Mr. Blanchard reviewed all assignments to ensure that Kevin was capable of completing them. Equipped with the information he needed, Mr. Blanchard met with the special education teacher, Ms. Johnson, to explore what might be done to help Kevin succeed in the classroom.
>
> Ms. Johnson observed Kevin in the classroom and then interviewed him to determine whether or not he knew and understood classroom rules. Convinced that Kevin did understand, Ms. Johnson and Mr. Blanchard developed a contract with Kevin: If he stayed in his seat, he could earn points toward a reward of his own choosing (15 minutes of computer time).
>
> Within a few weeks, Kevin had increased staying in his seat by about 20 percent, and he was completing 50 percent of his work.

If students with emotional and behavioral problems are to reach their full academic potential, it is essential to reduce the incidences of problematic behavior. For years, teachers and paraprofessionals have successfully applied behavioral management techniques to increase positive behaviors and to decrease inappropriate ones. As they have learned, the key to success is not to try to *control* behavior reactively, per se, but to *proactively manage it consistently and productively.*

Increasing Appropriate Behaviors

It is important to respond to student behavior in positive ways, and it is important to resist any temptation to focus only (or even predominantly) on the inappropriate behavior. The first step in modifying behavior is to identify the behavior that should occur instead of merely focusing on the inappropriate behavior. Once desirable behaviors are selected for reinforcement, the following strategies can be used to increase the likelihood that the student will use them.

Positive Reinforcement

Point systems, stickers, smiles, and public recognition for a job well done are all examples of positive reinforcement. When a desired behavior is followed by something that the student finds rewarding, the likelihood increases that the desired behavior will occur more often. Educators find that setting up positive consequences helps some students learn to use new behaviors. Consequences that are dependent upon the performance of appropriate behaviors (also known as "response contingencies") help students improve their behaviors, particularly when the student is not intrinsically motivated to change.

While many students are intrinsically rewarded by social recognition (e.g., adult or peer praise) for their appropriate behavior, other students will initially need tangible reinforcers, such as those described in Table 4.3. It is important, though, to pair these rewards with social reinforcement so that the social reinforcement will ultimately become rewarding and the tangible reinforcer can gradually be removed.

Table 4.3   How to Make the Transition From Tangible Reinforcers to Social Reinforcers

- Reinforce immediately (especially when working with new behaviors or young or immature students), as any delay may result in ambiguity over which behavior is being reinforced.
- If immediate reinforcement is not possible, acknowledge the behavior and remind the student that the reinforcement will be coming.
- Give a verbal description of the behavior being reinforced so that the student knows exactly which behaviors have led to the reward.
- Use social reinforcers (e.g., praise or recognition) and activity reinforcers (e.g., time on a computer) in conjunction with tangible ones.
- Phase out tangible and contrived reinforcers as soon as possible.
- Gradually increase the time between the behavior and the reinforcer.
- Be sensitive to peer pressure and be careful not to embarrass a student when presenting reinforcement.

A behavioral contract is a good example of making a reward depend upon a desired response. Most effective contracts usually contain (1) concrete definitions of expected behavior; (2) positive consequences for demonstrating expected behavior; (3) a statement of everyone's role (e.g.,

Negative Reinforcement

Negative reinforcement theory says that a student will perform appropriate behaviors to avoid or escape negative consequences. For example, students complete their homework to avoid failing, or students sit appropriately in order to stop a teacher from "nagging" them. Such strategies should be used sparingly because they focus attention on inappropriate behaviors. However, when they are used, they should always be paired with the reinforcement of an appropriate, alternative behavior (e.g., occasionally rewarding the student for sitting appropriately or for completing his or her homework). Students need to know what they *should* be doing, not just what will not be tolerated.

"Mr. Jameson will monitor the rate of homework completion during the duration of the contract"); and (4) a statement of commitment from everyone involved.

Token economies (point systems) are other examples of response contingencies. Within these systems, students are asked to perform appropriate behaviors for which they receive tokens (or points) to be exchanged later for a predetermined reward. As students become proficient in demonstrating acceptable behavior, points are given less frequently. When using point systems, it is sometimes useful for the student to see a visual chart that represents his or her progress toward reaching a goal.

Decreasing Inappropriate Behaviors

For most students, an increase in appropriate behaviors will replace the need for interventions that focus on decreasing inappropriate behaviors. However, some inappropriate behaviors may necessitate the use of "behavior-decreasing consequences."

Planned Ignoring

The use of planned ignoring ("extinction") is based upon the theory that if the inappropriate behavior is used to gain attention, ignoring the behavior will result in its becoming "extinct." Three points should be stressed when using extinction:

- The use of extinction is not recommended for behaviors that are unsafe or harmful.

- If the student is gaining desired attention from his or her peers, the behavior will not decrease unless peers also ignore it.

- Usually, a short-term consequence of extinction is that the targeted behavior *initially* tends to become worse before it becomes better.

Punishment

Punishment receives a great deal of attention. While occasionally it may be necessary to use punishment as a consequence for inappropriate behavior, it should be only a small part of a behavioral management plan. The theory behind punishment is that the behavior will decrease if it is followed by something the student perceives as negative. "Response cost" (e.g., losing points in a token economy) is an example of punishment.

There are three correlates to punishment: (1) punishment focuses on what the student *should not be doing* rather than on what he or she *should be doing;* (2) punishment often causes emotional reactions, not only from the student whose behavior is being punished, but from other students; and (3) punishment is often the result of student behaviors that are highly frustrating to educators, thus, it is important to react to frustrating behaviors in a calm and rational manner so as not to increase the student's negative behavior.

Using Punishment

Punishment should only be considered when:

- The behavior is dangerous to the student or others.
- Every other intervention has been appropriately implemented and has failed.
- The student's behavior is so noxious that it prevents him or her from learning or forming meaningful social relationships.

Time-Out

Time-out is an often misunderstood punishment technique that actually refers to "time-out from positive reinforcement." With time-out, all reinforcement ceases and the student is essentially removed from a reinforcing situation. It is especially effective for attention-seeking behaviors. For example, if a student makes inappropriate comments during small-group activities to get the other students to laugh, removing the student from the others in his or her group might be a good intervention.

Effective use of time-out requires discussing with the student in advance those behaviors that may lead to a time-out, as well as the proper procedures for going to, being in, and returning from time-out. Time-out, then, should be clearly differentiated from other removal techniques and from places students voluntarily go to when they feel they need time to gain control over themselves or their situation.

Effective time-out strategies incorporate a multilevel system of increasing seclusion. For example, a student first may be asked to put his or her head down; at the next level, the student might turn away from or leave the group; and finally, a separate location, or "seclusionary time-out," may be used when the intensity of the behavior warrants such removal.

The use of seclusionary time-out has caused some controversy. Critics charge it denies students their right to education, while serving as nothing more than a form of "imprisonment." As a result of such claims, some school districts have banned the use of seclusionary time-out. It is, therefore, best to consult school policies *before* implementing seclusionary time-out in the classroom. It is also a good idea to discuss the procedure with the child's IEP team prior to implementing such a technique. If school board policy allows seclusionary time-out, the facilities should be adequate and the time-outs well monitored, short in duration, and used judiciously. Each time a student is sent to time-out, ask yourself if the student is being denied an opportunity to learn while in seclusionary time-out. Table 4.4 contains guidelines for implementation of time-out procedures.

Table 4.4   Implementation Guidelines of Time-Out
• Consult school administration for district time-out policies.
• Discuss the use of time-out options and procedures with students' parents.
• Define which behaviors will earn time-out.
• Decide how long the time-out should last.
• Thoroughly discuss the time-out procedure with students.
• Specify the behaviors that warrant time-out.
• Specify the warnings to be given prior to time-out.
• Teach directions for going to time-out.
• Teach proper time-out behavior.
• Teach procedures for returning from time-out.
• Post time-out rules in the classroom.
• Warn students when their behavior may lead to time-out.
• Implement time-out without emotion or discussion.
• Begin timing the time-out only when the student begins to exhibit appropriate behavior.
• Discuss appropriate alternative behaviors in private upon student's return from time-out.
• Specify time-out procedures in the student's IEP.

For each incidence of seclusionary time-out, keep a time-out log that includes:

• Child's name

• Description of behavior or incident that resulted in time-out

• Time of incident

• Duration of time-out

• Behavior during time-out

Review the time-out log regularly to evaluate the effectiveness of the time-out procedures.

Teaching New Behaviors

Some students with learning difficulties do not learn appropriate behaviors by observation alone. Students may not be performing a particular behavior simply because they have not been taught it. In these cases, the behavior may not indicate defiance on the student's part, but simply the inability to behave in an appropriate manner. Such a situation may arise if certain social skills are required for the performance of a specific task (e.g., sharing or taking turns as lab partners in a science experiment). Many students with emotional and behavioral problems have never been taught *correct* social skills and, as a result, are at a distinct disadvantage in situations requiring any type of social interaction.

Once students have performed the new behavior with frequent success, a self-monitoring strategy can be introduced where students keep track of how often or how long they use the new behavior. Such strategies are used to help students manage and evaluate their own behavior.

Use the following instructional strategies to help teach students new behaviors:

- **Modeling:** Show the student the appropriate use of the behavior.

- **Rehearsing appropriate behavior:** Provide opportunities for the student to practice the behavior.

- **Role-playing:** Provide students the opportunity to practice the behavior in the context of a situation in which the behavior might be needed.

- **Continuous reinforcement:** Provide reinforcement to the student as he or she practices the new behaviors.

- **Prompting:** Give students cues to help them remember how and when to use the new behaviors.

Sometimes educators find that students need extra support to behave appropriately. Table 4.5 explains some "tricks of the trade" that are useful to support appropriate behaviors.

Teaching Social Skills

A growing trend in elementary schools is to teach social skills as part of regular classroom lessons. Teachers first identify necessary classroom social skills (such as waiting one's turn, sharing materials, saying "excuse me," listening, and following directions), then they select a particular skill and break it down into observable steps. They teach those steps, while modeling the behaviors themselves and asking students to do the same. Students also role-play the skill and receive positive feedback from the teacher, paraprofessional, and other students. Throughout the rest of the day, adults target naturally occurring opportunities to reinforce the students when they demonstrate their newly learned social skills.

Summary

A key to increasing appropriate behaviors and decreasing inappropriate ones is motivation. Through careful application of behavior management strategies, teachers and paraprofessionals can actually teach motivation and, hence, improve classroom behavior.

Strategies designed to manage behavior may be quite effective in the short run, but, by themselves, they are not sufficient to bring about long-term behavior change. Teachers and paraprofessionals who build positive relationships with students have the greatest chance of succeeding over time. Basic skills must be delivered within a *compassionate context*—a humane and safe environment filled with caring relationships. All students benefit from having caring adult educators in their lives. Both students and educators contend that such a person can, in fact, be the single most important component in helping anyone with emotional or behavioral problems take the first step toward adjustment. It is impossible to overemphasize the power of caring.

Table 4.5   Strategies to Support Appropriate Behavior

1. **Proximity control.** The educator uses his or her physical presence to reduce inappropriate behaviors and to increase appropriate ones. For example, if a student is staring out a window, the teacher can continue lecturing while moving toward the student in a nonthreatening way. The teacher's presence serves as a reminder to the student that he or she should be paying attention. The use of direct eye contact can be used to enhance this technique. It is important to remember that in emotionally charged situations, it is not good to get too close or make the student feel cornered.

2. **Signal interference.** Rather than use a direct warning to stop an inappropriate behavior and encourage a positive one, educators can signal, or prompt, a student by using a previously agreed upon sign. (This can be a private signal known only by the student and educator.) For example, teachers commonly put their index finger to their lips to indicate it is time to be quiet, or they tap a chime to alert students to stop what they are doing and face them.

3. **Redirection.** Teachers and paraprofessionals use redirection, when necessary, to verbally remind a student of the task at hand. For instance, if a student is out of his seat and wandering around, the paraprofessional might redirect the behavior by saying: "John, show me how many answers you've completed in your workbook." The redirective statement *positively* reminds John of what he *should* be doing, and it allows him to reengage in the learning activity without punishment.

4. **Relaxation.** When students are agitated, such as after a heated argument during recess, teachers can have them relax quietly by putting their heads on their desks. Similarly, when students feel upset, they can be taught to count backwards or breathe deeply before reacting. It is best, however, to teach students such techniques when they are calm. Educators also may enhance the success of these techniques by teaching students to recognize "triggers" of stress and anger (see Managing Aggressive Behaviors section of this chapter).

5. **Talking the student down.** If a student has become agitated but has not lost control, it may be useful to "talk the student down" to a more relaxed state. With this technique, the teacher or paraprofessional talks very calmly, slowly, and quietly to a student, leading him or her to a positive solution.

6. **Humor.** Sometimes potentially volatile behavior can be diffused by gently drawing attention to something funny about the situation that provoked the behavior. However, educators are cautioned against using sarcasm or trivializing a deeply felt emotion. It is important to maintain a mutually respectful relationship with the student.

Managing Aggressive Behaviors

Back early from lunch, Terrance storms into the classroom, knocking over desks and chairs. He swings at a stack of books sitting on the counter, sending them sailing across the room. The few students who also are back early begin moving quickly away from Terrance, hovering close to the teacher's desk and along the room's perimeter. Screaming "I hate you!" he lunges toward Bryan, who is racing toward the door.

Even when lessons are delivered effectively, a management system is in place, and rapport is established, it is still possible for acts of aggression to occur. When a student loses control in the classroom, it is the educator's primary responsibility to ensure the safety of everyone involved.

Usually, a student does not lose control without "giving notice." We understand from research that when students act out, their behavior follows a predictable pattern. In fact, one of the best lines of defense for classroom teachers and paraprofessionals is to understand the nature of this "acting-out behavior" pattern and to use that knowledge to support the student.

A student's sense of calm can become disrupted by certain environmental triggers, such as changes in routine, too many errors or corrections on assignments, or peer provocation. Triggers also can come from outside the classroom, stemming from such things as gang pressure, substance abuse, lack of sleep, and peer or family conflicts. There are some triggers that educators can control (e.g., preparing students for transition, ensuring a student takes his or her medication as scheduled, teaching anger management skills) and others that are beyond their control (e.g., an upheaval in the family, conflicts with friends). Providing a structured, supportive environment and teaching students anger management and problem-solving skills will reduce the impact of triggers on behavior.

When students are triggered, they usually become confused or defiant. They may ask lots of questions and begin arguing. Sometimes just showing interest in a student, or giving a student a chance to talk about what is bothering him or her, can help the student regain self-control or enable the educator to provide appropriate support. Provide the student with time and space at this point and allow him or her to work independently. Prompt the student to use relaxation skills and problem-solving skills to work through the anger. It is important to remain calm and to continue to treat the student with respect. If you become upset or rude, the student's behavior will only escalate. If the student's behavior continues to escalate, remind him or her in a respectful way of the consequences of the behavior. Give the student the opportunity to choose the appropriate behavior.

However, should a student loose control, the educator's priority is safety. This includes the safety of the others in the room as well as that of the student who is out of control. If the student's behavior is endangering others in the classroom, ask the student to leave the room. If the student refuses to leave, have the other students leave the room and send one student for help. In either case, tell the student(s) exactly where they should go and whom they should talk to. Again, remain calm and respectful so as not to escalate the behavior.

Following a loss of control, the teacher or paraprofessional should debrief with the student and help the student identify appropriate, alternative behaviors. This debriefing should be done when the student has calmed down and is receptive to working with an adult, and it should be approached as an opportunity for the student to learn. The issues of discipline and of consequences for the disruptive behavior should be broached separately.

Schools should take the time to develop emergency procedures in the event a student loses control and threatens the safety of other students. This plan should be taught and practiced before an incident occurs.

▪▪▪▪▪▪ Enlisting Help at School

Some students demand more attention and understanding than any one teacher or paraprofessional can give. It is rare that these students have problems with their behavior in only one setting (e.g., classroom, cafeteria, playground, or hallways). In such cases, colleagues work together to help support the student's behavioral growth. A behavior management plan, for instance, is more powerful if it is applied in more than one setting and by more than one adult. Essentially, schoolwide approaches are good ideas, as they can minimize environmental triggers, provide structure and consistency, and are more effective in addressing behavioral needs over the long run.

To be most effective, the entire school community and families must address violent and aggressive behavior; therefore, it is imperative to enlist the support and resources of all concerned. In response to this growing need, many schools are providing students with conflict resolution and peer mediation skills. Some schools are even adopting schoolwide social skills and discipline programs. Procedures should be in place for dealing with violent behavior and criminal actions in the school, because educators should not be left on their own to deal with such situations. Table 4.6 lists suggested criteria to follow when implementing a schoolwide plan.

Policies must be written down that state what is and is not allowable in a plan in order to avoid misconceptions. Once a plan is developed, staff must receive training about how to put the plan into effect, and they should conduct a review of its implementation after a practice run to evaluate the plan's effectiveness.

▪▪▪▪▪ Working Together With Families

Emotional and behavioral problems affect children in all life situations—home, community, school, church, etc. In addition, families experience significant stress when their children have emotional and behavioral problems, and they need to work with the schools to address the students' needs. Communication with the student's family should, therefore, be one of the *most important components* of any school program. Because a family unit may be configured in many ways, it frequently helps to know and refer to the significant members of a child's family (e.g., mother, father, grandparent, aunt, older sibling, other adult) and the role they play in the student's life. The core members of the family should be included in all significant deliberations about the student's education.

The IEP team offers opportunities to meet with the child's family. Collaboration can extend throughout the year, as family members are made to feel at home with teachers and professionals

Table 4.6   Criteria of a Schoolwide Behavior Management Plan

- Explain the purpose of the plan.

- State behavioral expectations.

- Explain strategies for teaching behavioral expectations to students.

- Include structures for reinforcing those students who demonstrate desired behaviors.

- Agree in advance on strategies for managing students who demonstrate problem behaviors.

- Include a continuum of backup consequences for students who resist efforts to change inappropriate behaviors.

- Outline a referral system (complete with strategies that educators use to document students who repeatedly demonstrate problem behavior). Also include a system for explaining *how* officials are to share information gathered via the plan with families, district officials, and, if appropriate, law enforcement officials.

- Include a step-by-step procedure for communicating the purpose of the schoolwide plan and the ways it will be used to address violence and criminal actions to parents and others.

charged with instructing their children. Meetings can be scheduled to facilitate family involvement and conducted in a manner that demonstrates respect for the student's family, their culture, and their knowledge and concerns. Empathy, respect, and sincerity are key factors in establishing and maintaining a positive relationship with families.

Because families like to hear good news, it is suggested that teachers and others share reports on student progress with families, either through notes, reward charts, completed contracts, phone calls, or record cards. In order to build trust and good support, it may be helpful to begin with positive examples of their child's performance or behavior before addressing inappropriate behaviors.

When talking to a family about the child's behavior in school, the following approaches may enlist the family's support:

- Refer to behavioral difficulties within the context of mastering academic goals.

- Be concrete and specific about behavior problems. Expressions that exaggerate the frequency of problem behaviors, such as "He *always* looks away when I smile at him," or "She talks back *all* of the time," serve only to make family members defensive.

- Actively listen to family members, empathize with their concerns, and learn from their knowledge and experience.

- Share positive examples of the student's performance and reaffirm a commitment to helping the student become successful in school.

- Solicit the family's suggestions concerning how to reduce inappropriate behaviors.

Moving Forward

While the characteristics presented by children with emotional and behavioral challenges may sometimes seem daunting, the bottom line is never to give up on *any* student. Because children with emotional and behavioral problems may challenge a teacher's patience and cause momentary despair, teachers need the support of others in helping students succeed.

The school is a learning community. While it is important to build a positive climate in the classroom, such work does not stop at the classroom door. The success of a classroom behavior management program can be enhanced by colleagues as well as by the student's family. In that spirit, the next chapter presents some promising practices that schools and districts are using to support classroom teachers and paraprofessionals.

School-Based
SUPPORTS

Both the middle schools and the high school in a northeastern school district employ collaborative teaching techniques among teams of regular and special educators. Coteaching teams modify instruction for individual students, while the school implements alternative disciplinary plans and establishes academic support centers that students throughout the school can utilize. These interventions have enhanced engagement and learning for all students—including those with emotional or behavioral challenges.

The district has supported these efforts by staffing the support centers with trained paraprofessionals, providing regular release time for collaborative teams of regular and special educators to meet and plan, and scheduling classes so that teaching teams share the same students.

In a southwestern school district, the school-based teacher assistance team has taken on a new role of coordinating professional development. Teachers, paraprofessionals, support service personnel, and administrators may request different staff development topics. The team analyzes these needs to design staff development opportunities that address both the topic in general and the particular needs of school personnel.

There is much that can be done in the classroom to provide high-quality educational programs to students with emotional and behavioral challenges. The school and district, however, must support such efforts. From this systemwide perspective, the goal is to build the school and district capacity to undertake the strategies and approaches that sustain and support positive results for all students, including students with emotional and behavioral problems.

When teachers and paraprofessionals serve as team members and are provided with adequate time to meet with the team, they are in an excellent position to solve problems or to identify resource needs. They can develop a rich understanding of their students' needs and share a stake in designing effective collaborative interventions that can help improve student learning and

This chapter describes some promising practices and approaches that are having a positive impact on students and classroom environments, such as:

- Reconfiguring services within and outside of the classroom and school

- Developing effective collaborative teams

- Offering professional development to all staff

An understanding of how these approaches support student progress enables teachers and paraprofessionals to seek out the approaches and advocate they be put into practice.

behavior. Teachers and paraprofessionals can play key roles in recommending the support services and resources that facilitate success in school.

Reconfiguring Services

Across the country, special services are being reconfigured to support students and educators. In some cases, social services are being brought to schools. In other cases, new concepts are being developed to address the emotional and behavioral needs of students. Here are four examples of redesigned service delivery models:

1. To support high school students with emotional and behavioral problems, educators in a Rhode Island district established a "planning room," wherein all students may find emotional support or extra help with schoolwork, do their homework in a quiet setting, or perform social problem-solving activities. A special education teacher—skilled in behavior management—supervises the planning room, tutors students in academic subjects, and helps students solve problems in socially appropriate ways. When a student needs additional help, such as community mental health services, the supervising teacher assists students in obtaining that help.

2. Educators in an Ohio district designed a plan that assigns special education paraprofessionals to regular education elementary classrooms where they work to provide academic and behavioral support directly to students. At the end of the day, the teacher, the paraprofessional, and individual students go over the progress made that day, and the students are invited to make suggestions on how they can improve the next day.

3. Social workers in a Michigan district are assigned to classrooms that include children with emotional and behavioral challenges. Then, as needed, they provide positive support to children in following classroom rules, solving problems, and developing positive attitudes.

4. Behavior specialists in a second Ohio district work with teachers who have students with behavior problems that exceed the teachers' skills for dealing with them. A behavior specialist consults with the teacher, observes the student, talks with the counselor and the parents, consults with the family physician (if necessary), and then develops a behavior management plan. The specialist works with the teacher to put the plan into place and is available to help on an on-call basis if the plan is not working.

These are just a few strategies schools have implemented to support the needs of both students and educators. In other cases, services that were once the sole province of "pull-out" settings (i.e., removing students from the classroom for services) are now being brought into the classroom. Teachers are becoming part of "coteaching partnerships," and some teachers have developed meaningful and productive new ways to include various service providers in the classroom program. For example, a behavior specialist might spend time each day assisting a student in the regular classroom, or the teacher of students with learning disabilities might coteach a lesson with the regular teacher to ensure that all students are challenged and no one is frustrated with the material.

Some school structures currently in place also are being revamped, with a special focus on supporting students with emotional and behavioral problems. Schoolwide behavioral management systems are being designed and implemented by entire school staffs, geared toward offering a consistent approach to supporting all students and to defining and communicating rules, expectations, and consequences.

Often, instructional components are built into such schoolwide behavior management systems to actually teach children self-control and social skills strategies. Individualized instructional support programs are sometimes offered that address the behavioral needs or skill deficits of children with emotional disturbance. In addition, school districts are starting to implement early intervention and prevention services for young children at risk of developing emotional or behavioral challenges, as well as transition services for older youth. Research suggests that all these services can enhance a student's intellectual and social development and allow successful adjustment into the world of work or further study.

It is helpful to find out about programs like these in your district or, when appropriate, employ or work with others to implement them. Educators can play a critical role in offering ideas for how new services can be developed or used in their particular classrooms and schools.

Alternative Settings

For the most part, the general education classroom is considered to be the most desirable environment for students. In particular, whenever possible, it is expected that students with disabilities will participate in the general curriculum, with appropriate aids and supports. Sometimes, however, students with emotional and behavioral challenges require more than reconfiguration of services in their current setting to achieve success in controlling or improving their behavior. In such cases, educators may make the decision that a student would be better served in an alternative setting.

Obviously, when that student is a child with a disability, all of the conditions required by the law must be met before the student may be placed there. An alternative setting could be a "school within a school" or it could be a separate school facility. The configuration of an alternative setting depends on what each community can provide, but it is best to keep students as close to the mainstream setting as is appropriate. This is because the goal of effective alternative programs should be to enable the students to get back to their original settings as soon as possible.

In the past, many alternative settings were thought of as custodial programs that served to "keep" students more than to educate them. Effective alternative programs now are more nurturing environments where trained personnel offer coordinated services that support students' return to their original settings. See Table 5.1, Selected Components of Effective Alternative Programs, for a detailed description of services that alternative programs should provide for students.

Developing Effective Collaborative Teams

Involving family members, other professionals, and the community in improvement efforts is the cornerstone of long-term change. Learning from colleagues and others is a tried-and-true way to

Table 5.1   Selected Components of Effective Alternative Programs

1. **A qualified staff.** The staff of alternative programs should be qualified, well trained, and experienced in teaching students with emotional and behavior problems. They should choose to teach in these settings and be present in sufficient numbers to guarantee a strong, positive adult presence. This ensures that students receive effective instruction and are understood by people who want to see them succeed.

2. **Availability of resources.** Alternative programs should have small class sizes; an emphasis on intensive instruction; effective and frequent communication among students, families, teachers, and other school staff; and sufficient social work, psychological, and counseling resources so that all students receive effective services.

3. **Functional assessment of student's skills.** An assessment should be performed to determine what each student needs, both academically and behaviorally—not what a particular curriculum says should be taught. Each assessment should be tailored to each individual child, rather than using a packaged assessment program. This kind of assessment aligns with what is required when preparing an IEP.

4. **Functional curriculum.** Based on the results of the individualized assessment, each student should have a functional curriculum that addresses his or her particular needs. In addition to appropriate academic instruction, the curriculum should be individualized to include instruction in whatever vocational, social, and life-training skills a student might need in order to function in the classroom. This curriculum should be written into a student's individualized plan of instruction.

5. **Effective and efficient instructional techniques.** The instructional strategies chosen to implement the student's curriculum should take into account how each child learns, such as considering a student's attention span or learning style. For example, a student may learn better when a direct instruction approach is used rather than he or she does in cooperative learning groups.

6. **Transition program.** Alternative programs should have a process in place to help students make the transition back to the regular program. Each student should begin this process as soon as the alternative program is initiated. Transition programs should address the skills each student needs to succeed in the regular setting or in a job.

7. **Comprehensive systems.** Alternative programs should work with community agencies that may also be providing services to the students as a system of care. Such agencies might include: children's mental health, social services, health services, foster care, juvenile justice, child protection services, and other services as outlined in Table 5.2. Working together to meet each student's spectrum of needs may improve the student's outcome both in and beyond school.

8. **Resources required by law and student IEPs to serve students with disabilities.** Alternative programs should have available the staff and resources necessary to provide access to the general curriculum and the supports and services necessary to provide students with disabilities an education that comports with the requirements of IDEA.

discover new ideas and approaches. Strategies for addressing the needs and strengths of students with emotional and behavioral problems can be identified through school-based student assistance teams; special and regular education teacher partnerships; and school, family, and community teams that include other service providers. With the new amendments to IDEA, regular and special education teachers are now partners in developing IEPs for all disabled students who are or may be participating in the regular education environment. This allows for enhanced collaboration among all parties.

Because the needs of students with emotional and behavioral challenges often transcend what schools are able to provide, community agencies increasingly play an important role in students' lives, making valuable linkages between schools and the community.

Linkages also can be developed where previously none existed. For example, teachers in one school were surprised to learn about the behavior specialist's availability to work with them inside their classrooms. After a planning day with the behavior specialist, during which teachers learned about what her services included, teachers scheduled her to conduct social skills activities in their classrooms. They also drew upon her expertise in including families in cooperative planning. In other situations, a school or community social worker or school psychologist may be able to provide similar services.

Teachers and paraprofessionals often report satisfaction with collaborative models, primarily citing the opportunity they provide to share knowledge, expand skills, and develop creative solutions to problems. At the same time, teachers stress that *time has to be made available on a regular basis* for such collaborations to be effective. In addition, districts need to reduce barriers to collaboration and introduce opportunities for professionals and families to meet or to integrate community service providers into the school setting to create a "system of care." (For information on specific resources, contact the CECP or the Center on Positive Behavioral Interventions and Support.) Table 5.2 details the components of a system of care and the services each component can provide to meet collaboration needs.

Providing Opportunities for Professional Development

Educators and related service providers alike want to ensure that students with emotional and behavioral difficulties receive the best education possible. School districts are discovering that effective professional development for educators can improve the education of these students. Teachers, paraprofessionals, parents, community members, administrators, and support staff— including bus drivers and cafeteria and playground monitors—should all work together. Everyone can benefit and improve his or her understanding of students with emotional and behavioral problems. Research has shown that to be maximally effective, professional development activities must have certain characteristics (see Table 5.3).

Moving Forward

Many students, at some time or another, present challenging behaviors. Therefore, classroom teachers and paraprofessionals are always on the front lines as they work to prevent inappropriate behaviors from interfering with students' academic progress. Clearly, helping students

Table 5.2   Components of a System of Care

1. Mental Health Services
  Prevention
  Early identification and
    intervention
  Assessment
  Outpatient treatment
  Home-based services
  Day treatment
  Emergency services
  Crisis residential services
  Therapeutic foster care
  Therapeutic group care
  Therapeutic camp services
  Residential treatment services
  Inpatient hospitalization

2. Social Services
  Financial assistance
  Home aid services
  Respite services
  Protective services
  Foster care
  Adoption

3. Educational Services
  Assessment and planning
  Classroom support
  Resource rooms
  Transition planning
  Self-contained special
    education
  Alternative programs
  Special schools
  Homebound instruction
  Residential schools

4. Health Services
  Health education and
    prevention
  Primary care
  Screening and assessment
  Early intervention
  Acute care
  Long-term care

5. Vocational Services
  Career education
  Vocational assessment

  Transition planning
  Job survival skills training
  Job coaching
  Vocational skills training
  Work experiences
  Job finding, placement, and
    retention services
  Supported employment

6. Recreational Services
  Mentoring
  After-school programs
  Summer camps
  Special recreation projects
  Youth development activities

7. Operational Services
  Case management
  Self-help and support groups
  Advocacy
  Transportation
  Legal services
  Volunteer programs

Note: See Appendix B for descriptions of all these services. **Source:** Adopted from *A System of Care for Severely Emotionally Disturbed Children and Youth* by B. A. Stroul and R. M. Friedman, 1986, rev. 1994. Washington, DC: CASSP Technical Assistance Center, Georgetown University Child Development Center.

Table 5.3   Selected Characteristics of Effective Professional Development

- Supply educators with research-based content knowledge about the subject.

- Give educators not only ideas for what to do, but provide them with information about why interventions work.

- Are intensive (i.e., time and training) and inclusive (i.e., support and resources) enough to produce a measurable change in students.

- Engage educators and give them skills to fine-tune what they have learned to fit their particular setting.

- Are sensitive to the unique needs of the school community and address the concerns of educators.

- Are conducted in a variety of formats to address individual learning needs.

manage their behaviors is a vital part of ensuring that they will not miss out on learning that will improve the quality of their lives. As the examples in this guidebook suggest, all of the following are needed to accomplish this:

- Comprehensive programs of schoolwide discipline expectations.

- Improved classroom management—using rules and procedures, teaching replacement behaviors, and implementing strategies that enhance acceptable behavior and reduce unacceptable behavior.

- Collaborative teaming to address the needs of students with low-level challenging behaviors.

- Emergency planning.

- High-quality alternative settings for students whose needs cannot be met in the regular classroom or neighborhood school to ensure that student learning and development continue to move forward.

Support and
RESOURCES

There is now much that teachers and paraprofessionals can do to support the educational development of students who face emotional and behavioral challenges, particularly since many of the techniques that work with these students can work with *all* students. This chapter contains organization names, descriptions of the kinds of resources the organizations provide, addresses, phone numbers (some that are toll free), fax numbers, e-mail addresses, and website addresses. These organizations are designed to assist people who are serving students with disabilities.

Organizations

Center for Effective Collaboration and Practice (CECP)

The Center is working to improve results for children and youth with, or at risk of developing, emotional and behavioral problems as well as their families. Its main goals are to identify effective practices and to disseminate this information to teachers, mental health professionals, Head Start personnel, juvenile justice personnel, child welfare professionals, family members, and others. To do this, CECP has put together a network of individuals and information sources that can aid educators in getting the help they need. CECP constantly updates its own records to ensure that its lists are current. In addition, CECP: (1) maintains e-mail-based listservs for teachers, school psychologists, emotional and behavioral disorder specialists, and those interested in issues of implementing IDEA; (2) offers author online discussions through its website; (3) maintains a database of relevant meetings and conferences on the website; and (4) helps to link individuals to service providers through its network of sites that engage in promising practices (called nurseries and greenhouses). The Center's website also provides access to free publications produced by CECP on many of the topics addressed in this document.

> **Center for Effective Collaboration and Practice**
> American Institutes for Research
> 1000 Thomas Jefferson Street NW, Suite 400
> Washington, DC 20007
> Phone: 202-944-5400
> Toll free: 888-457-1551
> Fax: 202-944-5454
> E-mail: center@air.org
> Internet: *www.air.org/cecp/cecp.html*

This chapter suggests additional organizations and resources that educators and school districts can use to assist them in improving the education of all students.

Center for the Study and Prevention of Violence (CSPV)

CSPV was established in 1992 to provide assistance toward understanding and preventing violence, particularly among adolescents. Since that time, CSPV has expanded its focus to include violence prevention throughout the life span. CSPV's research-to-practice efforts have resulted in the following services: (1) a collection of research literature and resources relating to the study and prevention of violence, (2) technical assistance for the development and evaluation of violence prevention and intervention programs, and (3) research analyses that focus on the causes of violence and the search for best practices to prevent violence.

> **Center for the Study and Prevention of Violence**
> Institute of Behavioral Science
> University of Colorado at Boulder
> Campus Box 442
> Boulder, CO 80309-0442
> Phone: 303-492-8465
> Fax: 303-443-3297
> Internet: *www.colorado.edu*

Blueprints for Violence Prevention

Blueprints for Violence Prevention is a collection of 10 violence prevention programs that the Center for the Study and Prevention of Violence determined has high scientific standards of program effectiveness. Blueprints includes a description of each of the selected violence prevention programs, including the theoretical rationale for the program, the program's core components for implementation, evaluation design and results, and practical experiences encountered during the program's implementation.

> **Blueprints for Violence Prevention**
> **Center for the Study and Prevention of Violence**
> Institute of Behavioral Science
> University of Colorado at Boulder
> 900 28th Street, Suite 107
> Campus Box 442
> Boulder, CO 80309
> Phone: 303-492-1032
> Fax: 303-443-3297
> E-mail: blueprints@colorado.edu
> Internet: *www.colorado.edu.cspv/blueprints*

Center on Positive Behavioral Interventions and Support

The Center on Positive Behavioral Interventions and Support was created through the U.S. Department of Education's Office of Special Education Programs to give schools capacity-building information and technical assistance for identifying, adapting, and sustaining effective schoolwide disciplinary practices. The Center aims to meet two goals: (1) to widely disseminate information concerning schoolwide positive behavioral interventions and supports to schools, families, and communities; and (2) to demonstrate to concerned parties at all levels (students, schools, districts, and states) that schoolwide positive behavioral interventions and supports are feasible and effective.

Center on Positive Behavioral Interventions and Support
5262 University of Oregon
Eugene, OR 97403-5262
Phone: 541-346-2505
Fax: 541-346-5689
E-mail: pbis@oregon.uoregon.edu
Internet: *www.pbis.org*

Council for Exceptional Children (CEC)

CEC is the largest international organization dedicated to improving educational outcomes for students with disabilities. The CEC holds international, state, and local conferences through its various chapters and produces a catalog of publications, available by calling 800-232-7323. It also maintains several ERIC Clearinghouses of information and research on education issues, accessible though the Internet.

Council for Exceptional Children
1920 Association Drive
Reston, VA 20191-1589
Phone: 703-620-3660
TTY: 703-264-9446
Fax: 703-264-9494
E-mail: cec@cec.sped.org
Internet: *www.cec.sped.org*

Council for Children with Behavioral Disorders (CCBD)

The CCBD, a division of the Council for Exceptional Children (CEC), is committed to promoting and facilitating the education and general welfare of children and youth with behavioral and emotional disorders. The CCBD publishes a research journal, *Behavioral Disorders;* a newsletter; and a practitioner-oriented magazine, *Beyond Behavior,* which are distributed to its members several times a year. The CEC may be contacted for information regarding CCBD's other publications as well as membership opportunities and regional and national conferences.

Council for Children with Behavioral Disorders
Internet: *www.ccbd.net*

Federation of Families for Children's Mental Health (FFCMH)

The Federation of Families for Children's Mental Health is a national, parent-run organization focused on the needs of children and youth with emotional, behavioral, or mental disorders and their families. The Federation has chapters in every state; holds regional and national meetings and events; provides technical assistance and materials; and publishes a newsletter, *Claiming Children.*

Federation of Families for Children's Mental Health
1021 Prince Street
Alexandria, VA 22314-2971
Phone: 703-684-7710
Fax: 703-836-1040
E-mail: ffcmh@crosslink.net
Internet: *www.ffcmh.org*

Institute on Violence and Destructive Behavior (IVDB)

The Institute on Violence and Destructive Behavior at the University of Oregon is an institute made up of University of Oregon faculty representing the schools of education, psychology, sociology, law, architecture, and public policy and planning. The Institute was created to address social problems of public concern; to focus, make accessible, and deliver expertise related to violence and destructive behavior; and to integrate IVDB's research, training, and service activities in these contexts. Its activities focus on research, instruction, and public service. One schoolwide violence prevention curriculum IVDB has implemented is Effective Behavior Support (EBS).

> **Institute on Violence and Destructive Behavior**
> 1265 University of Oregon
> Eugene, OR 97403-1265
> Phone: 541-346-3592
> E-mail: ivdb@darkwing.uoregon.edu
> Internet: *www.darkwing.uoregon.edu/~ivdb/index.html*

National Information Center for Children and Youth with Disabilities (NICHCY)

The National Information Center for Children and Youth with Disabilities is an information clearinghouse funded by the Department of Education. The Center provides information on disabilities and disability-related issues for children and youth (birth to age 22). Many of its documents are provided free of charge.

> **National Information Center for Children and Youth with Disabilities**
> P.O. Box 1492
> Washington, DC 20013-1492
> Toll free: 800-695-0285
> Fax: 202-884-8441
> E-mail: nichcy@aed.org
> Internet: *www.NICHCY.org*

National Association of School Psychologists (NASP)

The National Association of School Psychologists has more members than any association of school psychologists in the world. The goal of NASP is to promote effective, research-validated programs that facilitate the creation of healthy school environments, support independence, and maximize learning. Professional but caring service, reliable research, advocacy, and constant program evaluation are emphasized. NASP publishes a newspaper eight times a year as well as a quarterly journal. In addition to these, NASP publishes books, monographs, pamphlets, videos, papers, and fact sheets.

> **National Association of School Psychologists**
> 4340 East West Highway, Suite 401
> Bethesda, MD 20814-9457
> Phone: 301-657-0270
> Fax: 301-657-0275
> TDD: 301-657-4155
> Internet: *www.naspweb.org*

National Institute of Mental Health (NIMH)

The National Institute of Mental Health's mission is to diminish the burden of mental illness through research. The Institute is a branch of the National Institutes of Health (NIH), the primary federal agency for biomedical and behavioral research. Both NIMH and NIH serve under the U.S. Department of Health and Human Services.

National Institute of Mental Health
Neuroscience Center Building
6001 Executive Boulevard
Bethesda, MD 20892
E-mail: nimhinfo@nih.gov
Internet: *www.nimh.nih.gov/home.htm*

Office of Juvenile Justice and Delinquency Prevention (OJJDP)

The Office of Juvenile Justice and Delinquency Prevention is one of several bureaus that serves under the U.S. Department of Justice's Office of Justice Programs (OJP). The OJP was established in 1984 to develop the nation's capacity to prevent and control crime, improve the criminal and juvenile justice systems, increase knowledge about crime and related issues, and assist crime victims. OJJDP creates and funds programs that target such issues as gang violence and juvenile crime. With OJP, OJJDP forms partnerships among federal, state, and local governments to address these and other problems relating to youth violence in the United States.

Office of Juvenile Justice and Delinquency Prevention
810 7th Street NW
Washington, DC 20531
Phone: 202-307-5911
Fax: 202-307-2093
E-mail: askjj@ojp.usdoj.gov
Internet: *www.ojjdp.ncjrs.org*

Juvenile Justice Clearinghouse
P.O. Box 6000
Rockville, MD 20849-6000
Toll free: 800-638-8736
Fax: 301-519-5212
E-mail: askncjrs@ncjrs.org

Parent Advocacy Coalition for Educational Rights (PACER)

The Parent Advocacy Coalition for Educational Rights is a nonprofit, statewide organization created to improve and expand opportunities that enhance the quality of life for children and young adults with disabilities and their families. PACER offers a variety of programs that provide assistance for children with disabilities, from birth to adulthood, and for students and schools. The Coalition also offers technical assistance to parent centers both locally and nationally. PACER's goal is to make parents informed consumers—for the welfare of their children—by providing parents with knowledge of their rights and responsibilities, about laws and other resources pertaining to their special-needs children, and about their roles as parents.

Parent Advocacy Coalition for Educational Rights Center
4826 Chicago Avenue South
Minneapolis, MN 55417-1098
Phone: 612-827-2966

TTY: 612-827-7770
Toll free (in MN): 800-53-PACER
Internet: *www.pacer.org*

Associations of Service Providers Implementing IDEA Reforms in Education (ASPIIRE) Partnership, and IDEA Local Implementation by Local Administrators (ILIAD) Partnership

These two partnerships funded by the Office of Special Education Programs (OSEP) are composed of more than 15 educational and related service organizations. As a group, the member organizations of ASPIIRE and ILIAD collaborate to provide ideas, technical assistance, and other information to assist educators in the field to implement IDEA '97 effectively.

ASPIIRE and ILIAD Projects
Council for Exceptional Children
1920 Association Drive
Reston, VA 20191-1589
Toll free: 877-CEC-IDEA
TDD: 703-264-9480
Fax: 703-264-1637
E-mail: ideapractices@cec.sped.org
Internet: *www.ideapractices.org; www.ideapractices.org/aspiire.htm; www.ideapractices.org/iliad.htm*

OSEP also funds a partnership of family organizations, Families and Advocates Partnership for Education (FAPE) at the PACER Center; and a partnership of policymaker organizations, the Policy Maker Partnership (PMP) for Implementing IDEA '97 at the National Association of State Directors of Special Education (NASDSE).

══════ State Special Education Departments

The following addresses and telephone numbers are for the departments within each state that oversee special education programs. Most state special education departments have staff members who specialize in the needs of students with emotional and behavioral disabilities. These staff members should be able to provide you with information about resources in your state or where you can find information you are looking for. States usually have different descriptive terms for "emotional and behavioral disabilities," so it's important to know what the terms are in your state and that you are prepared to explain your question in detail.

Call the number of your state's special education department listed here, then ask to speak to the department that specializes in the needs of students with emotional and behavioral disabilities (using the appropriate terms for your state).

ALABAMA Department of Education
Special Education Services
Box 302101
Gordon Persons Building
Montgomery, AL 36130-2101
Phone: 334-242-8114
Fax: 334-242-9192

ALASKA Department of Education
Office of Special and Supplemental Services
801 West 10th Street, Suite 200
Juneau, AK 99801-1894
Phone: 907-465-8702
Fax: 907-465-3396

ARIZONA Department of Education
Exceptional Student Services
1535 West Jefferson
Phoenix, AZ 85007-3280
Phone: 602-542-4831
Fax: 602-542-5404

ARKANSAS Department of Education
Associate Director for Special Education
Room 105-C, Dept. of Education Building
4 State Capitol Mall
Little Rock, AR 72201-1071
Phone: 501-682-4221
Fax: 501-682-5159

CALIFORNIA Department of Education
Special Education Division
515 L Street, #270
Sacramento, CA 95814
Phone: 916-445-4602
Fax: 916-327-3706

COLORADO Department of Education
Special Education Services Unit
201 East Colfax Avenue
Denver, CO 80203
Phone: 303-866-6695
Fax: 303-866-6811

CONNECTICUT State Department of Education
Bureau of Special Education and Pupil Services
Division of Educational Programs and Services
25 Industrial Park Road
Middletown, CT 06457
Phone: 860-807-2025
Fax: 860-807-2047

DELAWARE Department of Education
Exceptional Children and Early Childhood Group
P.O. Box 1402
Dover, DE 19903-1402
Phone: 302-739-5471
Fax: 302-739-2388

DISTRICT OF COLUMBIA Public Schools
Associate Superintendent for Special Education
825 North Capitol Street NW, 6th Floor
Washington, DC 20003
Phone: 202-442-5511
Fax: 202-442-5517

FLORIDA Education Center
Bureau of Instructional Support and Community
Services
325 West Gaines Street, Suite 614
Tallahassee, FL 32399-0400
Phone: 850-488-1570
Fax: 850-921-8246

GEORGIA Department of Education
Division for Exceptional Students
1870 Twin Towers East
205 Butler Street
Atlanta, GA 33334-5040
Phone: 404-656-3963
Fax: 404-651-6457

HAWAII Department of Education
State Special Education Section
3430 Leahi Avenue
Honolulu, HI 96815
Phone: 808-733-4990
Fax: 808-733-4841

IDAHO State Department of Education
Special Education Section
P.O. Box 83720
Boise, ID 83720-0027
Phone: 208-332-6917
Fax: 208-334-4664

ILLINOIS State Board of Education
100 North 1st Street, Mail Code N-243
Springfield, IL 62777-0001
Phone: 217-782-3371
Fax: 217-524-6125

INDIANA Department of Education
Division of Special Education
State House, Room 229
Indianapolis, IN 46204-2798
Phone: 317-232-0570
Fax: 317-232-0589

IOWA Department of Public Instruction
Bureau of Children, Family, and Community
Services
Grimes State Office Building
Des Moines, IA 50319-0146
Phone: 515-281-4030
Fax: 515-242-6019

KANSAS State Department of Education
Student Support Services
120 SE 10th Avenue
Topeka, KS 66612-1182
Phone: 785-291-3097
Fax: 785-296-1413

KENTUCKY Department of Education
Division of Exceptional Children Services
500 Mero Street, Room 805
Frankfort, KY 40601
Phone: 502-564-4970
Fax: 502-564-6721

LOUISIANA Department of Education
Division of Special Populations
P.O. Box 94064, 9th Floor
Baton Rouge, LA 70801-9064
Phone: 225-342-3633
Fax: 225-342-5880

MAINE Department of Education
Special Services
Station 23
Augusta, ME 04333
Phone: 207-287-5950
Fax: 207-287-5900

MARYLAND State Department of Education
Division of Special Education
200 West Baltimore Street
Baltimore, MD 21201-2595
Phone: 410-767-0238
Fax: 410-333-8165

MASSACHUSETTS Department of Education
State Director for Special Education
Executive Director for Educational Improvement
350 Main Street
Malden, MA 02148-5023
Phone: 781-338-3300
Fax: 781-338-3396

MICHIGAN Department of Education
P.O. Box 30008
608 West Allegan Street
Lansing, MI 48909-7508
Phone: 517-373-9433
Fax: 517-373-7504

MINNESOTA Department of Children, Families,
and Learning
Division of Special Education
1500 Highway 36 West
Roseville, MN 55113-4266
Phone: 651-582-8289
Fax: 651-582-8729

MISSISSIPPI Department of Education
Bureau of Special Services
P.O. Box 771
359 North West Street
Jackson, MS 39205-0771
Phone: 601-359-3498
Fax: 601-359-2198

MISSOURI Department of Elementary and Special
Education
Division of Special Education
P.O. Box 480
Jefferson City, MO 65102-0480
Phone: 573-751-2965
Fax: 573-526-4404

MONTANA Division of Special Education
Office of Public Instruction
P.O. Box 202501
Helena, MT 59620-2501
Phone: 406-444-4429
Fax: 406-444-3924

NEBRASKA Department of Education
Special Populations Office
301 Centennial Mall South
P.O. Box 94987
Lincoln, NE 68509-4987
Phone: 402-471-2471
Fax: 402-471-5022

NEVADA Department of Education
Educational Equity
700 East 5th Street, Suite 113
Carson City, NV 89710-5096
Phone: 775-687-9171
Fax: 775-687-9123

NEW HAMPSHIRE Department of Education
Special Education Program Management Team
101 Pleasant Street
Concord, NH 03301-3860
Phone: 603-271-6693
Fax: 603-271-1953

NEW JERSEY Department of Education
Office of Special Education Programs
P.O. Box 500
Trenton, NJ 08625-0500
Phone: 609-633-6833
Fax: 609-984-8422

NEW MEXICO Department of Education
State Director of Special Education
300 Don Gaspar Avenue
Santa Fe, NM 87501-2786
Phone: 505-827-6549
Fax: 505-827-6791

NEW YORK State Education Department
Office for Special Education Services
1 Commerce Plaza, Room 1624
Albany, NY 12234-0001
Phone: 518-474-2714
Fax: 518-474-8802

NORTH CAROLINA Department of Public
Instruction
Exceptional Children Division
301 North Wilmington Street
Raleigh, NC 27601-2825
Phone: 919-715-1565
Fax: 919-715-1569

NORTH DAKOTA Department of Public
Instruction
Special Education
600 East Boulevard
Bismarck, ND 58505-0440
Phone: 701-328-2277
Fax: 701-328-4149

OHIO Department of Education
Division of Special Education
933 High Street
Worthington, OH 43085-4087
Phone: 614-466-2650
Fax: 614-728-1097

OKLAHOMA Department of Education
Special Education Services
2500 North Lincoln Boulevard
Oklahoma City, OK 73105-4599
Phone: 405-521-4868
Fax: 405-522-2066

OREGON Department of Education
Office of Special Education
255 Capitol Street NE
Salem, OR 97301-0203
Phone: 503-378-3598
Fax: 503-373-7968

PENNSYLVANIA Department of Education
Bureau of Special Education
333 Market Street, 7th Floor
Harrisburg, PA 17126-0333
Phone: 717-783-6913
Fax: 717-783-6139

RHODE ISLAND Department of Education
Office of Special Needs, Room 406
Shepard Building, 225 Westminster Street
Providence, RI 02903
Phone: 401-222-4600
Fax: 401-222-6030

SOUTH CAROLINA Department of Education
Office of Programs for Exceptional Children
Rutledge Building, Room 505
1429 Senate
Columbia, SC 29201
Phone: 803-734-8806
Fax: 803-734-4824

SOUTH DAKOTA Department of Education and
Cultural Affairs
Office of Special Education
700 Governors Drive
Pierre, SD 57501-2291
Phone: 605-773-3678
Fax: 605-773-6846

TENNESSEE Department of Education
Division of Special Education
Andrew Johnson Tower, 5th floor
710 James Robertson Parkway
Nashville, TN 37243-0380
Phone: 615-741-2851
Fax: 615-532-9412

TEXAS Education Agency
Special Education Unit
W.B. Travis Building, Room 6-127
1701 North Congress Avenue
Austin, TX 78701-1494
Phone: 512-463-9414
Fax: 512-463-9434

UTAH State Office of Education
At-Risk and Special Education Services
Special Education Services Unit
250 East 500 South
Salt Lake City, UT 84111-3204
Phone: 801-538-7711
Fax: 801-538-7991

VERMONT Department of Education
Family and Educational Support Team
120 State Street
Montpelier, VT 05620-2501
Phone: 802-828-5118
Fax: 802-828-3140

VIRGINIA Department of Education
Office of Special Education and Student Services
P.O. Box 2120
Richmond, VA 23216-2120
Phone: 804-225-2402
Fax: 804-371-8796

WASHINGTON Special Education Section
Superintendent of Public Instruction
Old Capitol Building
Olympia, WA 98504-0001
Phone: 360-753-6733
Fax: 360-586-0247

WEST VIRGINIA Department of Education
Office of Special Education
Building 6, Room B-304, Capitol Complex
1900 Kanawha Boulevard
Charleston, WV 25305
Phone: 304-558-2696
Fax: 304-558-3741

WISCONSIN Department of Public Instruction
Division for Learning Support, Equity, and
Advocacy
P.O. Box 7841
Madison, WI 53707-7841
Phone: 608-266-1649
Fax: 608-267-3746

WYOMING Department of Education
Special Education Unit
Hathaway Building, 2nd Floor
2300 Capitol Avenue
Cheyenne, WY 82002-0050
Phone: 307-777-7417
Fax: 307-777-6234

BUREAU OF INDIAN AFFAIRS
Branch of Exceptional Education
Mail Stop 3512/Mib Code 523
1849 C Street NW
Washington, DC 20240-4000
Phone: 202-208-5037
Fax: 202-208-5548

DEPARTMENT OF DEFENSE
Special Education Coordinator
Office of Dependents Education
4040 Fairfax Drive
Arlington, VA 22203
Phone: 703-696-4493
Fax: 703-696-8924

GUAM Department of Education
Division of Special Education
P.O. Box DE
Hagatna, GU 96932
Phone: 671-475-0549
Fax: 671-475-0562

PUERTO RICO Department of Education
Assistant Secretariat of Special Education
Hato Ray, PR 00919-0759
Phone: 787-753-7981
Fax: 787-753-7691

State Children's Mental Health Departments

The addresses and telephone numbers that follow are the children's mental health departments in each state that oversee the mental health programs for children. Most are part of their state's mental health department, but a few are connected with other agencies.

Staff members should be able to provide you with information about resources in your state. Call the number of your state's children's mental health department listed below. Explain the question that you have, then ask to speak to the person who can answer that question.

ALABAMA Department of Mental Health
and Mental Retardation
RSA Union Building, 100 North Union Street
Montgomery, AL 36130-1410
Phone: 334-242-3640
Fax: 334-242-0684

ALASKA Department of Health and Social Services
Division of Mental Health and Developmental Disabilities
P.O. Box 110620
Juneau, AK 99811-0620
Phone: 907-465-3370
Fax: 907-465-2668

ARIZONA Department of Health Services
Division of Behavioral Health Services
2122 East Highland, Suite 100
Phoenix, AZ 85016
Phone: 602-381-8999
Fax: 602-553-9140

ARKANSAS Department of Human Services
Division of Mental Health Services
4313 West Markham Street
Little Rock, AR 72205-4096
Phone: 501-686-9164
Fax: 501-686-9182

CALIFORNIA Department of Mental Health
Health and Welfare Agency
1600 9th Street, Room 151
Sacramento, CA 95814
Phone: 916-654-2309
Fax: 916-654-3198

COLORADO Department of Human Services
Division of Mental Health Services
3824 West Princeton Circle
Denver, CO 80236
Phone: 303-866-7401
Fax: 303-866-7428

CONNECTICUT Department of Mental Health and
Addictions Services
410 Capitol Avenue, MS#14COM
Hartford, CT 06106
Phone: 203-418-6700
Fax: 203-418-6691

DELAWARE Department of Health and Social
Service
Division of Alcoholism, Drug Abuse, and Mental Health
1901 North Dupont Highway
New Castle, DE 19720
Phone: 302-577-4461
Fax: 302-577-4484

DISTRICT OF COLUMBIA Commission on
Mental Health Services
4301 Connecticut Avenue NW, Suite 310
Washington, DC 20008
Phone: 202-364-3422
Fax: 202-364-4886

FLORIDA Department of Children and Families
Mental Health Program Office
1317 Winewood Boulevard
Building 3, Room 102
Tallahassee, FL 32399-0700
Phone: 904-488-8304
Fax: 904-487-2239

GEORGIA Department of Human Resources
Division of Mental Health, Mental Retardation, and Substance Abuse
2 Peachtree Street, Suite 22.224
Atlanta, GA 30303
Phone: 404-657-2260
Fax: 404-657-1137

HAWAII Department of Mental Health
Adult Mental Health Division
1250 Punchbowl Street, Room 256
P.O. Box 3378
Honolulu, HI 96801-3378
Phone: 808-586-4677
Fax: 808-586-4745

IDAHO Department of Health and Welfare
Bureau of Mental Health
450 West State, 7th Floor
Boise, ID 83720
Phone: 208-334-5528
Fax: 208-334-6699

ILLINOIS Department of Human Services
Office of Mental Health
400 William G. Stratton Building
Springfield, IL 62765
Phone: 217-782-7555
Fax: 217-785-3066

INDIANA Department of Family and Social Services
Division of Mental Health
402 West Washington Street, Room W-353
Indianapolis, IN 46204-2739
Phone: 317-232-7845
Fax: 317-233-3472

IOWA Department of Human Services
Division of Mental Health and Developmental
Disabilities
Hoover State Office Building
1305 East Walnut Street
Des Moines, IA 50319-0114
Phone: 515-281-5126
Fax: 515-281-4597

KANSAS Department of Social and Rehabilitation
Services
Division of Healthcare Policy
Docking State Office Building
915 SW Harrison Street, 5th Floor North
Topeka, KS 66612-1570
Phone: 913-296-3773
Fax: 913-296-5507

KENTUCKY Department of Mental Health and
Mental Retardation Services
100 Fair Oaks Lane
Frankfort, KY 40601-0001
Phone: 502-564-4527
Fax: 502-564-5478

LOUISIANA Department of Health and Hospitals
Office of Mental Health
1201 Capitol Access Road, 4th Floor
Baton Rouge, LA 70802
Phone: 504-342-9238
Fax: 504-342-5066

MAINE Department of Mental Health
Mental Retardation and Substance Abuse
Services
411 State Office Building, Station 40
Augusta, ME 04333
Phone: 207-287-4223
Fax: 207-287-4268

MARYLAND Department of Health and Mental
Hygiene
Mental Hygiene Administration
201 West Preston Street, Room 416A
Baltimore, MD 21201
Phone: 410-767-6613
Fax: 410-333-5402

MASSACHUSETTS Department of Mental Health
25 Staniford Street
Boston, MA 02114
Phone: 617-727-5600
Fax: 617-727-4350

MICHIGAN Department of Community Health
320 Walnut Street, Lewis Cass Building, 6th Floor
Lansing, MI 48913
Phone: 517-335-0196
Fax: 517-335-3090

MINNESOTA Department of Human Services
Mental Health Program Division
Human Services Building, 444 Lafayette Road
St. Paul, MN 55155-3828
Phone: 651-297-3510
Fax: 651-582-1831

MISSISSIPPI Department of Mental Health
    1101 Robert E. Lee Building
    239 North Lamar Street
    Jackson, MS 39201
    Phone: 601-359-1288
    Fax: 601-359-6295

MISSOURI Department of Mental Health
    1706 East Elm Street
    P.O. Box 687
    Jefferson City, MO 65101
    Phone: 573-751-3070
    Fax: 573-526-7926

MONTANA Department of Public Health and
    Human Services
    Addictive and Mental Disorders Division
    1400 Broadway, Room C118
    P.O. Box 202951
    Helena, MT 59620-2951
    Phone: 406-444-3969
    Fax: 406-444-4435

NEBRASKA Department of Health and
    Human Services
    P.O. Box 95044
    Lincoln, NE 68509
    Phone: 402-479-5117
    Fax: 402-479-5162

NEVADA Department of Human Services
    Division of Mental Health and Developmental
    Disabilities
    505 East King Street, Room 602
    Carson City, NV 89701-3790
    Phone: 775-684-5943
    Fax: 775-687-5966

NEW HAMPSHIRE Department of Health and
    Human Services
    Division of Behavioral Health and Developmental
    Disabilities
    State Office Park South, 105 Pleasant Street
    Concord, NH 03301
    Phone: 603-271-5007
    Fax: 603-271-5058

NEW JERSEY Department of Human Services
    Division of Mental Health Services
    50 East State Street, Capitol Center
    P.O. Box 727
    Trenton, NJ 08625
    Phone: 609-777-0702
    Fax: 609-777-0662

NEW MEXICO Department of Health Services
    Behavioral Health Services Division
    1190 St. Francis Drive, Room N3300
    Santa Fe, NM 87502
    Phone: 505-827-2601
    Fax: 505-827-0097

NEW YORK State Office of Mental Health
    44 Holland Avenue
    Albany, NY 12229
    Phone: 518-474-4403
    Fax: 518-474-2149

NORTH CAROLINA Department of Health and
    Human Resources
    Division of Mental Health
    Developmental Disabilities and Substance Abuse
    Services
    325 North Salisbury Street
    Raleigh, NC 27603
    Phone: 919-733-7011
    Fax: 919-733-9455

NORTH DAKOTA Department of Human Services
    Division of Mental Health and Substance Abuse
    Services
    600 South 2nd Street, Suite 1D
    Bismarck, ND 58504-5729
    Phone: 701-328-8941
    Fax: 701-328-8969

OHIO Department of Mental Health
    30 East Broad Street, 8th Floor
    Columbus, OH 43266-0414
    Phone: 614-466-2337
    Fax: 614-752-9453

OKLAHOMA Department of Mental Health
    and Substance Abuse Services
    1200 North East 13th Street
    Oklahoma City, OK 73117
    Phone: 405-522-3878
    Fax: 405-522-0637

OREGON Department of Human Resources
Mental Health and Developmental Disabilities
Division
2575 Bittern Street NE
Salem, OR 97310
Phone: 503-945-9499
Fax: 503-378-3796

PENNSYLVANIA Department of Public Welfare
Office of Mental Health and Substance Abuse
Services
Health and Welfare Building, Room 502
Commonwealth and Forster Streets
Harrisburg, PA 17120
Phone: 717-787-6443
Fax: 717-787-5394

RHODE ISLAND Department of Mental Health,
Mental Retardation, and Hospitals
14 Harrington Road
Cranston, RI 02920
Phone: 401-462-3201
Fax: 401-462-3204

SOUTH CAROLINA Department of Mental Health
2414 Bull Street, Suite 321
P.O. Box 485
Columbia, SC 29202
Phone: 803-898-8320
Fax: 803-898-8586

SOUTH DAKOTA Department of Human Services
Division of Mental Health
Hillsview Plaza
East Highway 34, c/o 500 East Capitol
Pierre, SD 57501-5070
Phone: 605-773-5991
Fax: 605-773-7076

TENNESSEE Department of Mental Health
and Mental Retardation
Cordell Hull Building, 3rd Floor
425 Fifth Avenue North
Nashville, TN 37243
Phone: 615-532-6500
Fax: 615-532-6514

TEXAS Department of Mental Health and Mental
Retardation
909 West 45th Street
Austin, TX 78751
Phone: 512-206-4588
Fax: 512-206-4560

UTAH Department of Human Services
Division of Mental Health
120 North 200 West, 4th Floor, Suite 415
Salt Lake City, UT 84103
Phone: 801-538-4270
Fax: 801-538-9892

VERMONT Department of Developmental and
Mental Health Services
103 South Main Street
Waterbury, VT 05671-1601
Phone: 802-241-2610
Fax: 802-241-1129

VIRGINIA Department of Mental Health
Mental Retardation and Substance Abuse Services
P.O. Box 1797, 109 Governor Street
Richmond, VA 23218
Phone: 804-786-3921
Fax: 804-371-6638

WASHINGTON Department of Social and Health
Services
Mental Health Division
P.O. Box 45320
14th and Jefferson Streets
Olympia, WA 98504
Phone: 360-902-0790
Fax: 360-902-7691

WEST VIRGINIA Department of Health and Human
Resources
Office of Behavioral Health Services
Capitol Complex, Building 6, Room B-717
Charleston, WV 25305
Phone: 304-558-0627
Fax: 304-558-1008

WISCONSIN Department of Health and Family
Services
Bureau of Community Mental Health
1 West Wilson Street
Madison, WI 53702
Phone: 608-267-9282
Fax: 608-267-7793

WYOMING Department of Health
Division of Behavioral Health
Hathaway Building, 1st Floor
2300 Capitol Avenue
Cheyenne, WY 82002
Phone: 307-777-7997
Fax: 307-777-5580

GUAM Department of Mental Health and Substance
Abuse
790 Governor Carlos C. Camacho Road
Tamuning, GU 96911
Phone: 671-647-5330
Fax: 671-647-6948

PUERTO RICO Mental Health and Anti-Addiction
Services
G.P.O. Box 21414
San Juan, PR 00928-1414
Phone: 787-758-0241
Fax: 787-765-7104

Materials for Further Study

A number of publications specifically address practitioners' questions about educating students
with emotional disturbance and behavioral problems. In general, these documents are not
reviewed to determine consistency with federal law or regulations. Nevertheless, here are a few
we believe are especially helpful:

Periodicals

The Journal of Emotional and Behavioral Problems: Reclaiming Children and Youth and *The
Journal of Emotional and Behavioral Disorders* are both published quarterly by:

Pro-Ed
8700 Shoal Creek Boulevard
Austin, TX 78757
Phone: 512-451-3246
Toll free: 800-897-3202

Preventing School Failure is published quarterly by:

Heldref Publications
1319 18th Street NW
Washington, DC 20036-1802
Phone: 202-296-6267
Toll free: 800-365-9753
Fax: 202-269-5149

Reaching Today's Youth: The Community Circle of Caring Journal, published quarterly by:

National Educational Service
1252 Loesch Road
P.O. Box 8, Station Z1
Bloomington, IN 47402-0008
Phone: 812-336-7700
Toll free: 800-733-6786
Fax: 812-336-7790

Local colleges and universities are also good resources. Many college and university libraries subscribe to research and practitioner journals that publish updated information on strategies for working with students with emotional and behavioral problems and their families. Education or school psychology departments often are aware of upcoming conferences and workshops.

Publications

CECP has produced a variety of products that may be of interest to teachers, paraprofessionals, administrators, and others on educational strategies for children and youth with emotional and behavioral problems. These are listed and described here, and most can be acquired free of charge. To obtain any of these materials, please contact CECP (unless otherwise indicated) using the information provided at the beginning of this chapter.

Early Warning, Timely Response: A Guide to Safe Schools. This document was produced in collaboration with NASP in response to the President's call for the development of an early warning guide to help "adults reach out to troubled children quickly and effectively." This guide has been distributed to every district in the nation to help them identify children in need of intervention into potentially violent emotions and behaviors. It can be acquired through the U.S. Department of Education by calling toll free at 877-4ED-PUBS or via the websites of the Office for Special Education Programs (*www.ed.gov/offices/OSERS/OSEP*) or CECP (*www.air.org/cecp*).

Safeguarding Our Children: An Action Guide. Since the U.S. Department of Education's release of the *Early Warning Guide,* the Department has received numerous requests for information on how schools can develop a comprehensive violence prevention plan. The *Action Guide* was written in response to that interest. It provides schools with practical steps to design and implement safety plans intended to reduce violence in our schools and to help children get the services they need. Twenty-five nationally known education and mental health organizations sponsored the *Action Guide.* It was released to all schools in the nation and can be acquired by calling toll free at 877-4ED-PUBS or via the websites of the Office for Special Education Programs (*www.ed.gov/offices/OSERS/OSEP*) or CECP (*www.air.org/cecp*).

Safe, Drug-Free, and Effective Schools for ALL Students: What Works! This report came out of a collaborative effort between the Office of Special Education Programs and the Safe and Drug-Free Schools Program, both of the U.S. Department of Education. It profiles six different approaches in three different communities or districts to address schoolwide prevention and the reduction of violent and aggressive behavior by all students. The report is the result of a literature review and focus groups comprised of students, families, administrators, teachers, and community-change agents from local agencies.

The Role of Education in a System of Care: Effectively Serving Children with Emotional and Behavioral Disorders. This is one of seven monographs prepared for the Center for Mental Health Services (CMHS) of the U.S. Department for Health and Human Services. It profiles effective school-based mental health systems of care. The information in this report was gathered through a series of site visits and focus groups, interviews, and a review of the literature. Seven additional monographs in this series on *Promising Practices in a System of Care* are also available by contacting CECP.

Addressing Student Problem Behavior: An IEP Team's Introduction to Functional Behavioral Assessment and Behavior Intervention Plans. Written with some of the country's leading experts, this document serves as a useful tool for educators to understand the requirements of IDEA '97 with regard to addressing behavior problems and implementing the fundamental principles and techniques of functional behavioral assessment and positive behavioral supports for students with behavior problems.

Addressing Student Problem Behavior, Part II: Conducting a Functional Assessment. The second document in the Addressing Student Problem Behavior Series, this monograph provides an in-depth discussion of the rationale for functional behavioral assessment and instructions for how to conduct the process. Sample forms are provided.

Addressing Student Problem Behavior, Part III: Creating Positive Behavioral Intervention Plans and Supports. The third document in the Addressing Student Problem Behavior Series, this monograph provides an in-depth discussion about creating and implementing positive behavior interventions and supports. It explains how to use the information gathered during the functional behavioral assessment process and how to develop and implement positive behavioral intervention plans.

Functional Assessment and Behavioral Intervention Plans: Part 1 is a two-hour video workshop on functional behavioral assessment. Produced as a cooperative effort between CECP and Old Dominion University (as part of the University's state-funded technical assistance project), it covers: (1) the definitions and origins of functional behavioral assessment, (2) what is involved in conducting a functional behavioral assessment and the criteria for determining when one is needed, and (3) other relevant issues surrounding this technique. It is available from the Training and Technical Assistance Center, Old Dominion University, 1401 West 49th Street, Norfolk, VA 23529-0146.

Functional Assessment and Behavioral Intervention Plans: Part II is a two-hour video workshop that builds on Part I to provide in-depth discussion of and instruction on how to conduct a functional behavioral assessment. It can be obtained by contacting Old Dominion University at the address above.

Supplemental Reading

Bristol, M. M. (1976). Control of physical aggression through school- and home-based reinforcement. In J. D. Krumholtz & C. E. Thoresen (Eds.), *Counseling methods* (pp. 180–186). New York: Holt.

Brophy, J. E. & Good, T. L. (1986). Teacher behavior and student achievement. In M. Wittrock (Ed.), *Handbook of research on teaching* (3rd ed., pp. 328–375). New York: MacMillan.

Canter, A. & Carroll, S. (Eds.). (1998). *Helping children at home and school: Handouts from your school psychologist.* Washington, DC: National Association of School Psychologists.

Carroll, S. (1998). Medical management of behavior and emotional problems in children and adolescents: A primer for educators. In A. Canter & S. Carroll (Eds.), *Helping children at home and school: Handouts from your school psychologist.* Washington, DC: National Association of School Psychologists.

Deitz, D. E. & Repp, A. C. (1983). Reducing behavior through reinforcement. *Exceptional Education Quarterly, 3,* 34–46.

Dunkin, M. & Biddle, B. (1974). *The study of teaching.* New York: Holt, Rinehart, and Winston.

Dwyer, K. & Osher, D. (2000). *Safeguarding our children: An action guide.* Washington, DC: U.S. Departments of Education and Justice, American Institutes for Research.

Dwyer, K., Osher, D., & Warger, C. (1998). *Early warning, timely response: A guide to safe schools.* Washington, DC: U.S. Department of Education.

Emmer, E. T., Evertson, C. M., & Anderson, L. M. (1980). Effective classroom management at the beginning of the school year. *The Elementary School Journal, 80*(5), 219–231.

Evertson, C., Anderson, C., Anderson, L., & Brophy, J. (1980). Relationships between classroom behaviors and student outcomes in junior high mathematics and English classes. *American Educational Research Journal, 7,* 43–60.

Gallagher, P. A. (1995). *Teaching students with behavior disorders.* Denver, CO: Love.

Goldstein, A. P. (1988). *The prepare curriculum.* Champaign, IL: Research Press.

Homme, L., Csanyi, A. P., Gonzales, M. A., & Rechs, J. R. (1970). *How to use contingency contracting in the classroom.* Champaign, IL: Research Press.

Hughes, C. A. & Hendrickson, J. M. (1987). Self-monitoring with at-risk students in the regular classroom setting. *Education and Treatment of Children, 10,* 236–250.

Hutchens, T. A., Canter, A., & Carroll, S. (1998). Medications for children with behavior and emotional problems: A primer for parents. In A. Canter & S. Carroll (Eds.), *Helping children at home and school: Handouts from your school psychologist.* Washington, DC: National Association of School Psychologists.

Johns, B. H. & Carr, V. G. (1995). *Techniques for managing verbally and physically aggressive students.* Denver, CO: Love.

Kazdin, A. E. (1994). *Behavior modification in applied settings* (5th ed.). Pacific Grove, CA: Brooks/Cole.

Kelley, M. L. & Stokes, T. F. (1982). Contingency contracting with disadvantaged youths: Improving classroom performance. *Journal of Applied Behavior Analysis, 15,* 447–454.

Kerr, M. M. & Nelson, C. M. (1989). *Strategies for managing behavior problems in the classroom* (3rd ed.). Upper Saddle River, NJ: Prentice-Hall.

Larrivee, B. (1985). *Effective teaching for successful mainstreaming.* New York: Longman.

Lochman, J. E. & Dodge, K. A. (1994). Social-cognitive processes of severely violent, moderately aggressive, and non-agressive boys. *Journal of Consulting and Clinical Psychology, 62,* 366–374.

Madsen, C. H. & Madsen, C. K. (1998). *Teaching discipline: A positive approach for educational development* (3rd ed.). Boston: Allyn & Bacon.

Mathur, S. R., Quinn, M. M., & Rutherford, R. B. (1995). *Teacher-mediated behavior management strategies for children with emotional and behavioral disorders.* Reston, VA: Council for Children with Behavioral Disorders.

McIntyre, T. (1992). The culturally sensitive disciplinarian. In R. B. Rutherford & S. R. Mathur (Eds.), *Severe behavior disorders of children and youth: Vol. 15. Monograph series in behavioral disorders* (pp. 107–115). Reston, VA: Council for Children with Behavioral Disorders.

Myles, B. S., Moran, M. R., Ormsbee, C., & Downing, J. A. (1992). Guidelines for establishing and maintaining token economies. *Intervention in School and Clinic, 27*(3), 164–169.

Office of Juvenile Justice and Delinquency Prevention (1995). *Guide for implementing the comprehensive strategy for serious, violent, and chronic juvenile offenders.* Washington, DC: Author.

Patterson, G. R., Reid, J. B., & Dishion, T. J. (1992). *Antisocial boys.* Eugene, OR: Castalia.

Premack, D. (1959). Toward empirical behavioral laws: Positive reinforcement. *Psychological Review, 66,* 219–221.

Rhode, G., Jenson, W. R., & Reavis, H. K. (1993). *The tough kid book: Practical classroom management strategies.* Longmont, CO: Sopris West.

Reid, R. (1993). Implementing self-monitoring interventions in the classroom: Lessons from research. In R. B. Rutherford & S. R. Mathur (Eds.), *Severe behavior disorders of children and youth: Vol 16. Monograph series in behavioral disorders* (pp. 43–54). Reston, VA: Council for Children with Behavioral Disorders.

Robins, L. N. & Ratcliff, K. S. (1978–79). Risk factors in continuation of childhood antisocial behaviors into adulthood. *International Journal of Mental Health, 7*(3–4), 96–116.

Rutherford, R. B., Chipman, J., DiGangi, S. A., & Anderson, K. (1992). *Teaching social skills: A practical instructional approach.* Ann Arbor, MI: Exceptional Innovations.

Rutherford, R. B. & Nelson, C. M. (1995). Management of aggressive and violent behavior. *Focus on Exceptional Children, 27,* 1–15.

Rutherford, R. B., Quinn, M. M., & Mathur, S. R. (1995). *Effective strategies for teaching appropriate behaviors to children with emotional and behavioral disorders.* Reston, VA: Council for Children with Behavioral Disorders.

Shapiro, E. S. & Cole, C. L. (1992). Self-monitoring. In T. H. Ollendick & M. Hersen (Eds.), *Handbook of child and adolescent assessment* (pp. 124–139). New York: Pergamon.

Shores, R. E., Gunter, P. L., Denny, R. K., & Jack, S. L. (1993). Classroom influences on aggressive and disruptive behaviors of students with emotional and behavior disorders. *Focus on Exceptional Children, 26,* 1–10.

Skiba, R. & Raison, J. (1990). Relationship between the use of timeout and academic achievement. *Exceptional Children, 57,* 36–46.

Spivack, G., Platt, J. J., & Shure, M. B. (1976). *The problem-solving approach to adjustment.* San Francisco: Jossey-Bass.

Sugai, G., Kameenui, E., & Colvin, G. (1993). *Project PREPARE: Promoting responsible, empirical, and proactive alternatives in regular education for students with behavior disorders.* Unpublished data, University of Oregon, College of Education.

Tharp, R. G. & Wetzel, R. J. (1969). *Behavioral modification in the natural environment.* New York: Academic Press.

Trice, A. D. & Parker, F. C. (1983). Decreasing adolescent swearing in an instructional setting. *Education and Treatment of Children, 6,* 29–35.

U.S. Congress. (1997). *Individuals with disabilities education act amendments.* Pub L No. 105–17 (Statute). Washington, DC: Author.

U.S. Department of Education. (1994). *National agenda for achieving better results for children and youth with serious emotional disturbance.* Washington, DC: Office of Special Education Programs, U.S. Department of Education.

U.S. Department of Education. (1999). *Assistance to states for the education of children with disabilities and the early intervention program for infants and toddlers with disabilities.* 48 Fed. Reg. 64 (to be codified at 34 CFR §300 and §303) (Final Regulations). Washington, DC: Author.

Walker, H. M. (1996). *The acting-out child: Coping with classroom disruption.* Longmont, CO: Sopris West.

Walker, H. M., Colvin, G., & Ramsey, E. (1995). *Antisocial behavior in school: Strategies and best practices.* Pacific Grove, CA: Brooks/Cole.

Walker, H. M. & Holland, F. (1979). Issues, strategies, and perspectives in the management of disruptive child behavior in the classroom. *Journal of Education, 161,* 25–50.

Walker, H. M., Shinn, M. R., O'Neil, R. E., & Ramsey, E. (1987). A longitudinal assessment of the development of antisocial behavior in boys: Rationale, methodology, and first year results. *Remedial and Special Education, 8,* 216–217.

Walker, H. M. & Walker, J. E. (1991). *Coping with noncompliance in the classroom: A positive approach for teachers.* Austin, TX: PRO-ED.

Ware, B. (1978). What rewards do students want? *Phi Delta Kappan, 59,* 355–356.

Yell, M. L. (1994). Timeout and students with behavior disorders: A legal analysis. *Education and Treatment of Children, 17,* 291–301.

Zaragoza, N., Vaughn, S. R., & McIntosh, R. (1991). Social skills interventions and children with behavior problems: A review. *Behavioral Disorders, 16,* 260–275.

IDEA '97

The Individuals with Disabilities Education Act Amendments of 1997 (Pub L No. 105–17): Sections of the law that pertain specifically to discipline of students with disabilities.

Readers may find the complete text of the Individuals with Disabilities Education Act (IDEA) statute and regulations, 34 CFR §300, in a variety of places, including on the websites of the U.S. Department of Education (*www.ed.gov/offices/OSERS/IDEA/*) and the Center for Effective Collaboration and Practice (*www.air.org/cecp/*).

Sec. 612(a)(22) SUSPENSION AND EXPULSION RATES

(A) IN GENERAL—The State educational agency examines data to determine if significant discrepancies are occurring in the rate of long-term suspensions and expulsions of children with disabilities—

(i)   among local educational agencies in the State; or

(ii)   compared to such rates for nondisabled children within such agencies.

(B) REVIEW AND REVISION OF POLICIES—If such discrepancies are occurring, the State educational agency reviews and, if appropriate, revises (or requires the affected State or local educational agency to revise) its policies, procedures, and practices relating to the development and implementation of IEPs, the use of behavioral interventions, and procedural safeguards, to ensure that such policies, procedures, and practices comply with this Act.

Sec. 613(j) DISCIPLINARY INFORMATION—

The State may require that a local educational agency include in the records of a child with a disability a statement of any current or previous disciplinary action that has been taken against the child and transmit such statement to the same extent that such disciplinary information is included in, and transmitted with, the student records of nondisabled children. The statement may include a description of any behavior engaged in by the child that required disciplinary action, a description of the disciplinary action taken, and any other information that is relevant to the safety of the child and other individuals involved with the child. If the State adopts such a policy, and the child transfers from one school to another, the transmission of any of the child's records must include both the child's current individualized education program and any such statement of current or previous disciplinary action that has been taken against the child.

Sec. 614(d)(3) DEVELOPMENT OF IEP

(B) CONSIDERATION OF SPECIAL FACTORS—The IEP Team shall—

(i)   in the case of a child whose behavior impedes his or her learning or that of others, consider, when appropriate, strategies, including positive behavioral interventions, strategies, and supports to address that behavior; . . .

(C) REQUIREMENT WITH RESPECT TO REGULAR EDUCATION TEACHER—
The regular education teacher of the child, as a member of the IEP Team, shall, to the extent appropriate, participate in the development of the IEP of the child, including the determination of appropriate positive behavioral interventions and strategies and the determination of supplementary aids and services, program modifications, and support for school personnel consistent with paragraph (1)(A)(iii).

Sec. 615(j) MAINTENANCE OF CURRENT EDUCATIONAL PLACEMENT—Except as provided in subsection (k)(7), during the pendency of any proceedings conducted pursuant to this section, unless the State or local educational agency and the parents otherwise agree, the child shall remain in the then-current educational placement of such child, or, if applying for initial admission to a public school, shall, with the consent of the parents, be placed in the public school program until all such proceedings have been completed.

Sec. 615(k) PLACEMENT IN ALTERNATIVE EDUCATIONAL SETTING—

(1) AUTHORITY OF SCHOOL PERSONNEL—

(A) School personnel under this section may order a change in the placement of a child with a disability—

(i) to an appropriate interim alternative educational setting, another setting, or suspension, for not more than 10 school days (to the extent such alternatives would be applied to children without disabilities); and

(ii) to an appropriate interim alternative educational setting for the same amount of time that a child without a disability would be subject to discipline, but for not more than 45 days if—

(I) the child carries a weapon to school or to a school function under the jurisdiction of a State or a local educational agency; or

(II) the child knowingly possesses or uses illegal drugs or sells or solicits the sale of a controlled substance while at school or a school function under the jurisdiction of a State or local educational agency.

(B) Either before or not later than 10 days after taking a disciplinary action described in subparagraph (A)—

(i) if the local educational agency did not conduct a functional behavioral assessment and implement a behavioral intervention plan for such child before the behavior that resulted in the suspension described in subparagraph (A), the agency shall convene an IEP meeting to develop an assessment plan to address that behavior; or

(ii) if the child already has a behavioral intervention plan, the IEP Team shall review the plan and modify it, as necessary, to address the behavior.

(2) AUTHORITY OF HEARING OFFICER—A hearing officer under this section may order a change in the placement of a child with a disability to an appropriate interim alternative educational setting for not more than 45 days if the hearing officer—

(A) determines that the public agency has demonstrated by substantial evidence that maintaining the current placement of such child is substantially likely to result in injury to the child or to others;

(B) considers the appropriateness of the child's current placement;

(C) considers whether the public agency has made reasonable efforts to minimize the risk of harm in the child's current placement, including the use of supplementary aids and services; and

(D) determines that the interim alternative educational setting meets the requirements of paragraph (3)(B).

(3) DETERMINATION OF SETTING—

(A) IN GENERAL—The alternative educational setting described in paragraph (1)(A)(ii) shall be determined by the IEP Team.

(B) ADDITIONAL REQUIREMENTS—Any interim alternative educational setting in which a child is placed under paragraph (1) or (2) shall—

(i) be selected so as to enable the child to continue to participate in the general curriculum, although in another setting, and to continue to receive those services and modifications, including those described in the child's current IEP, that will enable the child to meet the goals set out in that IEP; and

(ii) include services and modifications designed to address the behavior described in paragraph (1) or paragraph (2) so that it does not recur.

(4) MANIFESTATION DETERMINATION REVIEW—

(A) IN GENERAL—If a disciplinary action is contemplated as described in paragraph (1) or paragraph (2) for a behavior of a child with a disability described in either of those paragraphs, or if a disciplinary action involving a change of placement for more than 10 days is contemplated for a child with a disability who has engaged in other behavior that violated any rule or code of conduct of the local educational agency that applies to all children—

(i) not later than the date on which the decision to take that action is made, the parents shall be notified of that decision and of all procedural safeguards accorded under this section; and

(ii) immediately, if possible, but in no case later than 10 school days after the date on which the decision to take that action is made, a review shall be conducted of the relationship between the child's disability and the behavior subject to the disciplinary action.

(B) INDIVIDUALS TO CARRY OUT REVIEW—A review described in subparagraph (A) shall be conducted by the IEP Team and other qualified personnel.

(C) CONDUCT OF REVIEW—In carrying out a review described in subparagraph (A), the IEP Team may determine that the behavior of the child was not a manifestation of such child's disability only if the IEP Team—

(i) first considers, in terms of the behavior subject to disciplinary action, all relevant information, including—

(I) evaluation and diagnostic results, including such results or other relevant information supplied by the parents of the child;

(II) observations of the child; and

(III) the child's IEP and placement; and

(ii) then determines that—

(I) in relationship to the behavior subject to disciplinary action, the child's IEP and placement were appropriate and the special education services, supplementary aids and services, and behavior intervention strategies were provided consistent with the child's IEP and placement;

(II) the child's disability did not impair the ability of the child to understand the impact and consequences of the behavior subject to disciplinary action; and

(III) the child's disability did not impair the ability of the child to control the behavior subject to disciplinary action.

(5) DETERMINATION THAT BEHAVIOR WAS NOT MANIFESTATION OF DISABILITY—

(A) IN GENERAL—If the result of the review described in paragraph (4) is a determination, consistent with paragraph (4)(C), that the behavior of the child with a disability was not a manifestation of the child's disability, the relevant disciplinary procedures applicable to children without disabilities may be applied to the child in the same manner in which they would be applied to children without disabilities, except as provided in section 612(a)(1).

(B) ADDITIONAL REQUIREMENT—If the public agency initiates disciplinary procedures applicable to all children, the agency shall ensure that the special education and disciplinary records of the child with a disability are transmitted for consideration by the person or persons making the final determination regarding the disciplinary action.

(6) PARENT APPEAL—

(A) IN GENERAL—

(i) If the child's parent disagrees with a determination that the child's behavior was not a manifestation of the child's disability or with any decision regarding placement, the parent may request a hearing.

(ii) The State or local educational agency shall arrange for an expedited hearing in any case described in this subsection when requested by a parent.

(B) REVIEW OF DECISION—

(i) In reviewing a decision with respect to the manifestation determination, the hearing officer shall determine whether the public agency has demonstrated that the child's behavior was not a manifestation of such child's disability consistent with the requirements of paragraph (4)(C).

(ii) In reviewing a decision under paragraph (1)(A)(ii) to place the child in an interim alternative educational setting, the hearing officer shall apply the standards set out in paragraph (2).

(7) PLACEMENT DURING APPEALS—

(A) IN GENERAL—When a parent requests a hearing regarding a disciplinary action described in paragraph (1)(A)(ii) or paragraph (2) to challenge the interim alternative educational setting or the manifestation determination, the child shall remain in the interim alternative educational setting pending the decision of the hearing officer or until the expiration of the time period provided for in paragraph (1)(A)(ii) or paragraph (2), whichever occurs first, unless the parent and the State or local educational agency agree otherwise.

(B) CURRENT PLACEMENT—If a child is placed in an interim alternative educational setting pursuant to paragraph (1)(A)(ii) or paragraph (2) and school personnel propose to change the child's placement after expiration of the interim alternative placement, during the pendency of any proceeding to challenge the proposed change in placement, the child shall remain in the current placement (the child's placement prior to the interim alternative educational setting), except as provided in subparagraph (C).

(C) EXPEDITED HEARING—

(i) If school personnel maintain that it is dangerous for the child to be in the current placement (placement prior to removal to the interim alternative education setting) during the pendency of the due process proceedings, the local educational agency may request an expedited hearing.

(ii) In determining whether the child may be placed in the alternative educational setting or in another appropriate placement ordered by the hearing officer, the hearing officer shall apply the standards set out in paragraph (2).

(8) PROTECTIONS FOR CHILDREN NOT YET ELIGIBLE FOR SPECIAL EDUCATION AND RELATED SERVICES—

(A) IN GENERAL—A child who has not been determined to be eligible for special education and related services under this part and who has engaged in behavior that violated any rule or code of conduct of the local educational agency, including any behavior described in paragraph (1), may assert any of the protections provided for in this part if the local educational agency had knowledge (as determined in accordance with this paragraph) that the child was a child with a disability before the behavior that precipitated the disciplinary action occurred.

(B) BASIS OF KNOWLEDGE—A local educational agency shall be deemed to have knowledge that a child is a child with a disability if—

(i) the parent of the child has expressed concern in writing (unless the parent is illiterate or has a disability that prevents compliance with the requirements contained in this clause) to personnel of the appropriate educational agency that the child is in need of special education and related services;

(ii) the behavior or performance of the child demonstrates the need for such services;

(iii) the parent of the child has requested an evaluation of the child pursuant to section 614; or

(iv) the teacher of the child, or other personnel of the local educational agency, has expressed concern about the behavior or performance of the child to the director of special education of such agency or to other personnel of the agency.

(C) CONDITIONS THAT APPLY IF NO BASIS OF KNOWLEDGE—

(i) IN GENERAL—If a local educational agency does not have knowledge that a child is a child with a disability (in accordance with subparagraph [B]) prior to taking disciplinary measures against the child, the child may be subjected to the same disciplinary measures as measures applied to children without disabilities who engaged in comparable behaviors consistent with clause (ii).

(ii) LIMITATIONS—If a request is made for an evaluation of a child during the time period in which the child is subjected to disciplinary measures under paragraph (1) or (2), the evaluation shall be conducted in an expedited manner. If the child is determined to be a child with a disability, taking into consideration information from the evaluation conducted by the agency and information provided by the parents, the agency shall provide special education and related services in accordance with the provisions of this part, except that, pending the results of the evaluation, the child shall remain in the educational placement determined by school authorities.

(9) REFERRAL TO AND ACTION BY LAW ENFORCEMENT AND JUDICIAL AUTHORITIES—

(A) Nothing in this part shall be construed to prohibit an agency from reporting a crime committed by a child with a disability to appropriate authorities or to prevent State law enforcement and judicial authorities from exercising their responsibilities with regard to the application of Federal and State law to crimes committed by a child with a disability.

(B) An agency reporting a crime committed by a child with a disability shall ensure that copies of the special education and disciplinary records of the child are transmitted for consideration by the appropriate authorities to whom it reports the crime.

(10) DEFINITIONS—For purposes of this subsection, the following definitions apply:

(A) CONTROLLED SUBSTANCE—The term "controlled substance" means a drug or other substance identified under schedules I, II, III, IV, or V in section 202(c) of the Controlled Substances Act (21 U.S.C. 812[c]).

(B) ILLEGAL DRUG—The term "illegal drug"—

(i) means a controlled substance; but

(ii) does not include such a substance that is legally possessed or used under the supervision of a licensed health-care professional or that is legally possessed or used under any other authority under that Act or under any other provision of Federal law.

(C) SUBSTANTIAL EVIDENCE—The term "substantial evidence" means beyond a preponderance of the evidence.

(D) WEAPON—The term "weapon" has the meaning given the term "dangerous weapon" under paragraph (2) of the first subsection (g) of section 930 of title 18, United States Code.

GLOSSARY OF TERMS USED IN TABLE 5.2

The following is a glossary of terms used in Table 5.2, Components of a System of Care, on page 46. Here, terms are listed in alphabetical order under each system component. The definitions were gathered from these sources:

Bruns, B. J. & Goldman, S. K. (Eds.). (1999). Promising practices in wraparound for children with serious emotional disturbance and their families. *Systems of care: Promising practices in children's mental health, 1998 Series, Volume 4.* Washington, DC: Center for Effective Collaboration and Practice, American Institutes for Research.

Butts, J. A., Snyder, H. N., Finnegan, T. A., Aughenbaugh, A. L., and Poole, R. S. (1996). *Juvenile court statistics, 1993.* Washington, DC: Office of Juvenile Justice and Delinquency Prevention. (Available online at *www.rtc.pdx.edu/resource/terms.htm.*)

Center for Substance Abuse Treatment. (1994). *Juvenile justice treatment planning chart.* Rockville, MD: Department of Health and Human Services.

Education Week on the Internet. (1999). Glossary. *Editorial projects in education.* (Available online at *www.edweek.org/context/glossary/glossary.htm.*)

Research and Training Center on Family Support and Children's Mental Health. (1994). *Glossary of children's mental health terms.* Portland, OR: Author, Portland State University. (Available online at *www.rtc.pdx.edu/resource/terms.htm.*)

Stroul, B. A. & Friedman, R. M. (1994). *A system of care for severely emotionally disturbed children and youth.* (Rev. ed). Washington, DC: CASSP Technical Assistance Center, Georgetown University Child Development Center.

1. Mental Health Services

Assessment. A process that results in an opinion about a child's mental or emotional capacity and that may include recommendations about treatment or placement.

Crisis residential services. Residential treatment services that aim to intervene in the crisis at hand and transition the child or youth back into his or her home and community.

Day treatment. Day treatment programs provide education, counseling, and family interventions during the entire day to a child or youth, who then returns to his or her caregiver in the evening.

Early identification and intervention. Treatment for emotional and behavioral problems that begins early in the course of the problem, with the goal of lessening the duration and severity of the problem.

Emergency services. Emergency services range from prevention efforts to crisis stabilization and are provided by a variety of agencies. Examples include hotlines and shelters for those in need of crisis intervention or emergency care.

Home-based services. Home-based services are delivered to children and youth and their families in a family's home. One goal is to emphasize the needs of the whole family, not just an individual within the family.

Inpatient hospitalization. Inpatient services that provide medical intervention for a child's or youth's emotional or behavioral problem.

Outpatient treatment. Outpatient treatment includes mental health services available in non-residential settings, such as mental health clinics, hospital outpatient departments, or community health centers.

Prevention. The goal of prevention is to reduce the occurrence of emotional problems in children and youth and their families who have not yet been identified as having emotional problems, particularly those who may be at risk.

Residential treatment services. Residential treatment services are delivered in a facility that offers 24-hour residential care, as well as treatment and rehabilitation or short-term crisis intervention.

Therapeutic camp services. In therapeutic camp programs, participants and staff live together in a rustic situation, which places more expectations for responsible and independent behavior on the campers than more traditional residential settings might.

Therapeutic foster care. Treatment and care for children and youth by trained families in the private homes of foster parents.

Therapeutic group care. Treatment for children and youth that includes a variety of interventions and is provided in homes with other children or youth.

2. Social Services

Adoption. In contrast to temporary care, adoption is intended to be a permanent placement. It is designed for those situations in which return to the biological parents is unlikely for a child or youth.

Financial assistance. Financial assistance from sources including local and federal governments to help families pay for necessities, such as food, clothing, and shelter.

Foster care. Foster care includes the placement of children in foster family homes, group homes, group child care facilities, and residential treatment centers because of abuse, neglect, or abandonment.

Home aid services. Services provided in the home, usually by nonprofessionals.

Protective services. Protective services are intended to prevent and protect children and youth from neglect, abuse, and exploitation by offering social services to identified or at-risk children and youth and their families.

Respite services. Temporary care given to an individual for the purpose of providing a period of relief to the primary caregivers. Respite is used to decrease stress in the homes of persons with disabilities or handicaps, thereby increasing caregivers' overall effectiveness.

3. Educational Services

Alternative programs. Alternative programs include a wide range of settings and are thus difficult to define. Not all children served in these programs are formally identified as having a disability. The advantage offered by alternative education programs is flexibility for students who have difficulty functioning in the regular classroom setting and/or are at risk for dropping out.

Assessment and planning. Techniques used to identify and determine placement of children in special education programs. Assessment is done using a variety of methods and measures. Planning for a student assessed and identified with a disability includes the development of an individual educational program (IEP).

Classroom support. In the past, most students with emotional and behavioral challenges were educated in separate classrooms and separate schools. However, new knowledge about educational and behavior management strategies and supports, along with safer and more effective medication, have made it possible to educate many of these students in the regular classroom, with appropriate supports and services. These supports and services include, among others, positive behavioral interventions, counseling, and assignment of paraprofessionals.

Homebound instruction. With this option, the school district arranges for the child to receive instruction at home.

Residential schools. Residential schools stress educational achievement for students with emotional and behavioral problems and are often located outside of a child's home community.

Resource rooms. A setting within the regular school where students with disabilities may receive educational services from a special education teacher (and teachers' aids, when available) for one or two instructional periods each day.

Self-contained special education. Full-time placement in a special education classroom in which a special educator (and teachers' aids, when available) provides intensive, structured academic and behavioral support and supervision.

Special schools. Nonresidential programs that provide a full-day educational program for children within a setting that is separate from the regular school.

Transition planning. When students with disabilities are 14 years old, their postsecondary plans should begin to take shape. IEPs should contain the coursework and services needed to work toward those postsecondary plans. (See also Vocational Services.)

4. Health Services

Acute care. Care for children who are injured or become ill. Services are usually provided on an outpatient basis.

Early intervention. Treatment for health problems that could lead to emotional or behavioral challenges that begins early on, once the problems have been identified through screening and assessment.

Health education and prevention. Educational programs aimed at promoting both physical and mental health as well as educating students about public health issues, such as sex education or substance abuse.

Long-term care. Services for children with chronic illnesses and their families. Children and youth receiving long-term care for their health problems also may require services from schools.

Primary care. Complete health examinations and follow-up care by physicians during a child's growth and development.

Screening and assessment. Evaluation to identify potential health problems early and to determine an appropriate course of treatment and service delivery.

5. Vocational Services

Career education. Designed to prepare students to enter the working world, career education programs teach students about types of careers, how to choose a career, skills and approaches that may be useful, and what to expect in working with an employer and other employees.

Job coaching. Assisting new employees meet the challenges and problems of a job, and acting as the communication liaison between the employee and employer.

Job finding, placement, and retention services. Provides services such as interviewing skills or other vocational services to help youth find job opportunities, apply for jobs, and maintain their employment over time.

Job survival skills training. Programs that teach youth how to maintain and succeed at their jobs. The skills covered often include training in social skills for appropriate interaction with others, taking criticism from employers, managing frustration, and meeting deadlines and staying on schedule.

Supported employment. An alternative to traditional full- or part-time employment for youth who need assistance making the transition to these kinds of jobs. Through supported employment programs, a youth has a paying job and the support of an adult to help him or her acquire and use the skills he or she needs to maintain the position.

Transition planning. When students with disabilities are 16 years old, their IEPs should contain the agency contacts that will need to be in place for their postsecondary plans. (See also Educational Services.)

Vocational assessment. An evaluation process for determining a youth's ability, career interests, and readiness for employment.

Vocational skills training. Training in more technical vocational skills includes instruction in fields like technology or in industries such as auto maintenance, childcare, or hospitality.

Work experience. Some programs organize vocational training and work experience opportunities for older youth to build their skill sets as well as their confidence.

6. Recreational Services

After-school programs. Programs that typically offer students a place to do their homework, with the support of program staff and opportunities to participate in extracurricular activities, such as art, music, or sports, in a supervised setting between the close of the school day and the evening.

Mentoring. Programs, such as Big Brothers/Big Sisters, that match a child or youth who could benefit from positive recreational and learning experiences with constructive role models.

Special recreation projects. Projects designed to help children and youth learn and enjoy a new activity.

Summer camps. Held during the summer for a limited number of days or weeks, summer camps provide children and youth with the opportunity to learn new skills, enjoy recreational activities, and interact with adults and peers outside the school setting. Summer camps may operate as a day camp program or as an overnight, residential program.

Youth development activities. Activities intended to develop positive behavior characterized by character, good citizenship, and leadership in children and youth.

7. Operational Services

Advocacy. The process of actively supporting the cause of an individual (case advocacy) or group (class advocacy), or speaking or writing in favor of, or on behalf of, an individual or group.

Case management. A service that helps clients obtain and coordinate community resources, such as income assistance, education, housing, medical care, treatment, vocational preparation, and recreation.

Legal services. Legal assistance is given in situations that cannot be settled through alternative resolution methods. Legal services are commonly retained in cases where a child might be removed from his or her home or when a youth becomes involved in the juvenile justice system.

Self-help and support groups. Groups that provide emotional support and help for dealing with a problem that members or their family members share, such as alcoholism, substance abuse, or extreme anxiety or anger.

Transportation. Many children and their families have difficulty accessing programs and services because they lack transportation to and from the locations where services are offered.

Volunteer programs. Volunteers organized to serve in a variety of roles, such as acting as a Big Brother/Big Sister or tutor, helping a youth find a job, or assisting in a classroom as a teacher's aide.